How to Be Happier

How to Be Happier
Paul Jenner

For UK order enquiries: please contact Bookpoint Ltd,
130 Milton Park, Abingdon, Oxon OX14 4SB.
Telephone: +44 (0) 1235 827720. Fax: +44 (0) 1235 400454.
Lines are open 09.00–17.00, Monday to Saturday, with a 24-hour
message answering service. Details about our titles and how to
order are available at www.teachyourself.com

For USA order enquiries: please contact McGraw-Hill Customer
Services, PO Box 545, Blacklick, OH 43004-0545, USA.
Telephone: 1-800-722-4726. Fax: 1-614-755-5645.

For Canada order enquiries: please contact McGraw-Hill Ryerson
Ltd, 300 Water St, Whitby, Ontario L1N 9B6, Canada.
Telephone: 905 430 5000. Fax: 905 430 5020.

Long renowned as the authoritative source for self-guided
learning – with more than 50 million copies sold worldwide –
the Teach Yourself series includes over 500 titles in the fields of
languages, crafts, hobbies, business, computing and education.

British Library Cataloguing in Publication Data:
a catalogue record for this title is available from the British Library.

Library of Congress Catalog Card Number: on file.

First published in UK 2007 by Hodder Education, part of Hachette
UK, 338 Euston Road, London NW1 3BH.

First published in US 2007 by The McGraw-Hill Companies, Inc.

This edition published 2010.

Previously published as *Teach Yourself Happiness*

The Teach Yourself name is a registered trade mark of
Hodder Headline.

Typeset by Macmillan Publishing Solutions.

Printed in Great Britain for Hodder Education, an Hachette UK
Company, 338 Euston Road, London NW1 3BH, by CPI Cox &
Wyman, Reading, Berkshire RG1 8EX.

The publisher has used its best endeavours to ensure that the URLs
for external websites referred to in this book are correct and active
at the time of going to press. However, the publisher and the
author have no responsibility for the websites and can make no
guarantee that a site will remain live or that the content will remain
relevant, decent or appropriate.

Hachette UK's policy is to use papers that are natural, renewable
and recyclable products and made from wood grown in sustainable
forests. The logging and manufacturing processes are expected to
conform to the environmental regulations of the country of origin.

Impression number   10 9 8 7 6
Year   2014 2013 2012 2011

This book is dedicated to those millions of people all over the world who refuse to do anything to make other people unhappy.

Acknowledgements

A very special thank you to Victoria Roddam, my editor at Hodder Education.

Contents

Meet the author

Welcome to *How to Be Happier!*

More than 20 years ago I read some words that significantly changed my life. These words were:

> *In what situation do I experience the maximum satisfaction of my whole being?*

They were spoken by the Norwegian philosopher Arne Naess during an interview with the magazine *Resurgence*. Naess was explaining his belief that we should all be asking deeper questions about the things that make us happy.

There's nothing controversial in those 13 words. They're not even particularly original. And yet they struck me with the force of a physical blow. Here was somebody raising the bar to a new and yet, surely, attainable level. *Maximum* satisfaction. *Whole* being.

Suddenly I had a new perspective on life. The things that had been preoccupying me had almost instantly become trivial. I now wanted nothing less than the qualities about which Naess spoke. I, too, wanted to experience the maximum satisfaction of my whole being. And not just once. I wanted to experience it every day, for as much of the day as possible.

I now began to question everything I was doing. Is *this* going to give me the maximum satisfaction of my whole being? If not, then I would no longer do it – unless, of course, it was something essential. I was now rejecting things that *didn't* measure up. That was relatively easy. But I still had to find those things that *did* cause the maximum satisfaction of my whole being. And so began a quest that has so far lasted two decades and which is still going on.

I'm not going to tell you the things I found. They're personal to me and yours will be personal to you. But I can tell you *how* I found them. I found them by 'running away'. By that I mean I left behind the things that were not making me happy and I opened myself to the possibility of all kinds of new experiences that *might*. I didn't follow a specific pre-planned trajectory. How could I, after all, predict which of many different things would make me happy if I hadn't yet experienced them? I had to leave it to chance, while giving chance the greatest possible scope to achieve success. Some of the things I discovered *were* predictable, but many came as a considerable surprise. And they surprise me still.

I've talked so far about the importance of 'external' things, things that would act on me from outside to 'make' me happy. But during my quest I discovered something else vitally important. I discovered that the amount of satisfaction external things gave me very much depended on the development of my 'internal' *ability* to be happy. Just as a person who has not developed the ability to read cannot derive pleasure from a book, so a person who has not fully developed the capacity for happiness cannot derive the maximum possible satisfaction from anything.

So, very soon my quest included throwing myself at the feet of those people who might be able to help me develop my latent *internal* abilities. I now knew that happiness was, to some extent, a skill and they showed me how to learn it.

This book is the result of those two parallel strands of enquiry, the external and the internal.

Paul Jenner
Spain, 2010

Only got a minute?

▶ There is no single cause of happiness – to be happier you need to work on several areas at once.

▶ In a world in which there are more and more causes of unhappiness, happiness requires a conscious effort.

▶ Taking control of your mind is a vital step towards greater happiness. You must eradicate the following ten negative ways of thinking: comparing with others; greed; an all-or-nothing attitude; perfectionism; exaggeration of problems; jumping to negative conclusions without good reason; allowing negative emotions to overrule logical thought; labelling yourself and others; doing things you 'should' rather than things that make you happy; taking responsibility for things that aren't your responsibility at all.

▶ You should also eradicate the following ten negative emotions: anger, blame, cynicism, hate, revenge, jealousy, resentment, suspicion, indifference, guilt.

▶ 'Eat happiness' by making sure your food contains the eight amino acids (isoleucine, leucine, lysine, methionine, phenylalanine, threonine, tryptophan, and valine) that can't be manufactured by the body, plenty of whole grains, vegetables, fruits, nuts and seeds. Minimize trans-fatty acids, saturated fats and omega-6 polyunsaturated fatty acids (PUFAs). Maximize monounsaturated fats and omega-3 PUFAs.

▶ Meditate for at least 20-minutes every day to access your inner reservoir of happiness.

▶ Produce your own 'happiness drugs' through exercise – exercise is at least as effective as antidepressants, but without the side effects.

▶ You can't be truly happy unless you feel free to be yourself. Express your unique personality in every way you can.

▶ Cultivate good relationships through acceptance – accept your partner, relatives and friends as they are.

▶ If you have a partner, enjoy monogamous sex four times a week or more – research shows that's the optimum for happiness for both men and women. Sex boosts dopamine, phenylethylamine (PEA) and oxytocin, all of which are important 'happy chemicals'.

▶ Do a 'good deed' every day – research shows that altruism boosts happiness.

5 Only got five minutes?

1 How happy are you?

▶ *In our society, in which we're subject to so many pressures, the first step is to take back control of personal happiness. Treat happiness as a challenge and make it your priority.*

▶ How to Be Happier *can help you if you're unhappy, or not as happy as you'd like to be, but if you're suffering from depression your first step should be to speak to your GP.*

▶ *You can make happiness the point of your life with a clear conscience, because when you're happy you're far more likely to help others than if you feel low.*

▶ *Work on both your internal and external happiness to achieve the optimum level of happiness.*

▶ *Here's something to do right now. Start a happiness diary.*

2 Building a happy brain

▶ *Your brain can be moulded almost like a muscle into the 'happy brain' you desire. One form of 'happiness exercise' is to eliminate your negative thoughts and permit only positive thoughts.*

▶ *Avoid these styles of thinking:*

　1 *Theirs is better. (comparing)*
　2 *I want more... and more. (greed)*
　3 *If it's not black, it must be white. (all-or-nothing)*
　4 *If it's not perfect, it's no good. (perfectionism)*

5 *Why is this always happening to me? (exaggeration)*
6 *I'm not going to like this. (jumping to negative conclusions)*
7 *I feel it, so it must be true. (emotional reasoning)*
8 *I'm a label; you're a label. (labelling)*
9 *I should do this; you should do that. (obligation)*
10 *If it's wrong, it must be my fault. (wrongly taking responsibility)*

There are also at least ten harmful emotions to avoid:
1 *anger*
2 *blame*
3 *cynicism*
4 *hate*
5 *hostility*
6 *revenge*
7 *jealousy*
8 *resentment*
9 *suspicion*
10 *indifference.*

Negative or positive attitudes develop in infancy. The four basic kinds of attitude are:
1 *I'm all right and you're all right.*
2 *I'm all right but you're not all right.*
3 *I'm not all right but you're all right.*
4 *I'm not all right and you're not all right.*

For maximum happiness, your thinking style needs to be number one.

---

3 Think yourself happy

We'll now look in more detail at those ten negative ways of thinking.

THEIRS IS BETTER (COMPARING)

Ignore advertising and don't make comparisons with the very rich. Instead, compare with the 10.5 million people in Britain who can't afford treats for themselves, and the 37 million Americans who live below the official poverty line.

I WANT MORE… AND MORE (GREED)

If you're the sort of person who always wants more and more, then you may be financially successful, but you'll never be truly happy. For a month, see how you get on without buying anything expensive and concentrating instead on life's free or inexpensive pleasures.

IF IT'S NOT BLACK, IT MUST BE WHITE (ALL-OR-NOTHING)

This is a style of thinking that keeps life simple but makes no allowance for real life's infinite shades of grey. Most of the time this mentality leads to a good deal of misery. Start looking for the grey instead.

IF IT'S NOT PERFECT, IT'S NO GOOD (PERFECTIONISM)

Perfectionism is striving for a mythical level that can't actually be attained by anyone. The end result is always unhappiness. Strive for a high level, but not perfection.

WHY IS THIS ALWAYS HAPPENING TO ME? (EXAGGERATION)

You may focus too much on the negative and exaggerate the significance of anything that goes wrong. Instead, look for the positive in every situation.

I'M NOT GOING TO LIKE THIS (JUMPING TO NEGATIVE CONCLUSIONS)

If you always jump to negative conclusions, you'll make yourself miserable. Instead, believe the best until you have concrete proof otherwise.

I FEEL IT, SO IT MUST BE TRUE (EMOTIONAL REASONING)

Feeling a failure doesn't make you a failure. Next time you have feelings that undermine your self-esteem, write them down. Then try to analyse the situation objectively with the help of a friend.

I'M A LABEL; YOU'RE A LABEL (LABELLING)

Labels like 'I'm a loser' or 'he's an idiot' can make life simpler, but they take no account of change and can become self-fulfilling prophecies. Don't use them.

I SHOULD DO THIS; YOU SHOULD DO THAT (OBLIGATION)

Doing what you allegedly 'should' isn't the same as doing what makes you happy. In future, attach more weight to happiness than to 'should'.

IF IT'S WRONG, IT MUST BE MY FAULT (WRONGLY TAKING RESPONSIBILITY)

Accepting responsibility for things that aren't your responsibility is a common error, especially among women. You'll be happier if you let other people take responsibility for themselves.

Once you've mastered the new positive thought patterns, try applying them to your past as well. You'll find that things that have been bothering you, no longer seem so bad.

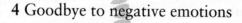

4 Goodbye to negative emotions

▶ *Anger is the opposite of what's needed for happiness. It can make you ill. When you feel angry with someone, protect your peace of mind and happiness with empathy – that's to say, imaginatively enter into the other person's situation. You won't feel angry any more.*

▶ *Release your stress not by shouting but by laughing.*

▶ *Remember: nobody has really failed until they give up – so don't give up.*

5 Eating happiness

▶ *The food you eat can affect your level of happiness.*

▶ *'Happy' foods include: alcohol in moderation, brazil nuts; coffee; chilli peppers; chocolate; complex carbohydrates in general; green leafy vegetables and legumes; garlic; oats; oysters; tea; wheatgerm.*

▶ *'Happy' food supplements include: folic acid (folate); selenium; zinc.*

▶ *Certain foods can cause allergic reactions in susceptible individuals, resulting in low moods.*

6 Inner happiness

▶ *External happiness is something you, and others, can create. Inner happiness is more like a reservoir that can be accessed through meditation.*

▶ *To meditate you can sit in: the classic lotus position, the half-lotus, cross-legged, in a chair or even lie down.*

▶ *A simple way of meditating involves slowing your breathing, making your exhalations longer than your inhalations, relaxing your mouth into a smile and emptying your mind.*

7 How to get happy-fit

▶ *Exercise increases your body's production of 'happy chemicals' and is as effective as antidepressants in combating depression. Even ten minutes of vigorous exercise is highly beneficial.*

▶ *It can be difficult to keep motivated, so it's important to find something you enjoy doing and that isn't expensive.*

▶ *Keep an exercise diary and reward yourself when you reach certain targets.*

8 Be happy being yourself

▶ *If you can't be yourself, you can't be truly happy; make your own path.*

▶ *Ask yourself: In what situation do I experience the maximum satisfaction of my whole being?*

▶ *It's important to be able to say 'no', but it's also important to learn to say 'yes' – it's usually the things we don't do that cause us the most regret.*

▶ *Learn to weigh up things in terms of happiness.*
  Ask yourself:
    ▷ *Is this likely to make me happy at any time?*
    ▷ *Is this likely to make me unhappy at some other time?*

9 Relationships, love and happiness

▶ *Connection equals happiness.*
▶ *A pet can increase your happiness.*
▶ *Try to love people the way you love your pet – that is, unconditionally.*
▶ *Don't project your fantasies onto other people – accept them as they really are.*

- ▶ Don't play 'mind games' with people – be straightforward and honest.
- ▶ Make up your mind that if you're going to have a relationship, then you're going to make it a great relationship.

10 Happy sex

- ▶ Studies show that frequent sex in a monogamous relationship promotes happiness equally in both men and women.
- ▶ In order to experience 'happy sex' to the full, both sexes need to get rid of inhibitions, introduce spirituality and develop the capacity for multiple orgasms.

11 Connection equals happiness

- ▶ As the biologist J.B.S. Haldane once observed: 'The universe is not only queerer than we suppose, it is queerer than we can suppose.'
- ▶ One of the queerest things about it is that everything is connected. Build on that connection by doing things to make the world a better place for everyone.

12 Your seven-day happiness plan

For the next seven days, conduct your life in accordance with the following eight principles:

1 *Start the day right.*
2 *Be positive.*
3 *No negatives.*

4 *Express yourself.*
5 *Improve your relationships.*
6 *Look after the physical.*
7 *Look after the spiritual.*
8 *Review the day.*

10 Only got ten minutes?

1 How happy are you?

▶ *Treat happiness as a challenge, just like learning a foreign language, mastering the lotus position or climbing a mountain. It calls for single-mindedness and, quite often, the setting aside of other less important goals. To be happy you have to make happiness your priority. Choose to be happy.*

▶ *If you're unhappy, or not as happy as you'd like to be, this book can help you. How to Be Happier may also help you if you're suffering from depression, but depression is a specific condition that needs specialist attention and your first step should be to speak to your GP.*

▶ *Remember that your happiness does not detract from anybody else's life. On the contrary, you're far more likely to help others when you feel happy than if you feel low. You can make happiness the point of your life with a clear conscience.*

▶ *Does true happiness come from within or without? It's a popular debating point but, in reality, it's a pointless question. You need to work on both your internal and external happiness to achieve the optimum level of happiness.*

▶ *Here's something to do right now. Start a happiness diary. As you try out the various ideas in this book, make a note of how well they work for you. Also note the times you feel happy and, if you can work it out, the cause of that happiness.*

2 Building a happy brain

▶ *There are physical differences between 'happy brains' and 'unhappy brains'. Fortunately, your brain remains 'plastic' all through your life, which means it can be moulded almost like a muscle into the 'happy brain' you desire. In other words, you can carry out exercises to transform your brain. One form* of 'happiness exercise' is to eliminate your negative thoughts and permit only positive thoughts.

▶ *There are ten different categories of negative thoughts that can make you unhappy and which you should therefore avoid. These are:*

1 *Theirs is better. (comparing)*
2 *I want more… and more. (greed)*
3 *If it's not black, it must be white. (all-or-nothing)*
4 *If it's not perfect, it's no good. (perfectionism)*
5 *Why is this always happening to me? (exaggeration)*
6 *I'm not going to like this. (jumping to negative conclusions)*
7 *I feel it, so it must be true. (emotional reasoning)*
8 *I'm a label; you're a label. (labelling)*
9 *I should do this; you should do that. (obligation)*
10 *If it's wrong, it must be my fault. (wrongly taking responsibility)*

These ten negative ways of thinking will be examined in more detail in the next section.

▶ *There are also, at least, ten harmful emotions to avoid. These are:*

1 *anger*
2 *blame*
3 *cynicism*
4 *hate*
5 *hostility*
6 *revenge*
7 *jealousy*
8 *resentment*
9 *suspicion*
10 *indifference.*

▶ *Negative or positive attitudes develop in infancy.*
In fact, according to many psychologists, infants very quickly develop into one of four types, rather entertainingly expressed like this:

1 *I'm all right and you're all right.*
2 *I'm all right but you're not all right.*
3 *I'm not all right but you're all right.*
4 *I'm not all right and you're not all right.*

For maximum happiness, your thinking style needs to be number one.

3 Think yourself happy

We'll now look in more detail at those ten negative ways of thinking. Remember, you are what you think. Think exclusively happy thoughts and you'll become a profoundly happy person.

THEIRS IS BETTER (COMPARING)

Advertisers want you to compare your lifestyle and possessions not just with the Joneses, but with the wealthiest people on the planet. None of us will ever be that rich, so we'll always be dissatisfied. The answer is to ignore those images. If you're going to compare, then compare with the 10.5 million people in Britain who can't afford to save or even spend small amounts on treats for themselves and the 37 million Americans who live below the official poverty line.

I WANT MORE... AND MORE (GREED)

Having insufficient money to meet the bills and pay for a few of life's little pleasures is clearly a cause of *un*happiness. But, beyond that, there's little evidence that increasing amounts of wealth lead to increasing amounts of happiness. If you're the sort of person who always wants more, then you may be financially successful, but you'll never be truly happy. For a month, see how you get on without buying anything expensive, and concentrating instead on life's free or inexpensive pleasures such as friendship, pets, nature, cycling in the countryside and identifying the stars.

IF IT'S NOT BLACK, IT MUST BE WHITE (ALL-OR-NOTHING)

This is a style of thinking that keeps life simple but makes no allowance for life's infinite shades of grey. Most of the time this mentality leads to a good deal of misery. If you're not a great success then you must be a failure. If you're not renowned as a great raconteur then you must be a bore.

For a change, try looking for the grey. For example, think of something in which you've always considered yourself hopeless. Then ask yourself: Have I really had adequate training? Have I really practised? Have I spent sufficient time trying? The answer is probably no. So you can't really say you're hopeless, can you?

IF IT'S NOT PERFECT, IT'S NO GOOD (PERFECTIONISM)

Perfectionism is something more than being conscientious, meticulous and painstaking. It's striving for a mythical level that can't actually be attained by anyone. Look around you. If something is perfect then it cannot be improved. Can you really see anything that couldn't be improved in any way? Striving for perfection wastes time and, quite often, makes it impossible to do anything at all. The end result is always unhappiness. Strive for a high level by all means, but not perfection.

WHY IS THIS ALWAYS HAPPENING TO ME? (EXAGGERATION)

You may focus too much on the negative and exaggerate the significance of anything that goes wrong. The whole thing is summed up in that well-known phrase: Why is this *always* happening to me? In fact, what makes us notice the things that go wrong, is not that they always happen, but that they happen so seldom. Instead of focusing on the negative, look for the positive in every situation.

I'M NOT GOING TO LIKE THIS (JUMPING TO NEGATIVE CONCLUSIONS)

When we don't know what's going on there's a tendency to jump to negative conclusions. Two people whispering together in a corner? They must be saying something horrible about me. A medical test? The result is bound to be serious. Making negative predictions is a recipe for anxiety and unhappiness. Believe the best, until you have concrete proof otherwise.

I FEEL IT, SO IT MUST BE TRUE (EMOTIONAL REASONING)

Feeling a failure doesn't make you a failure. Emotions are not necessarily a reliable guide to reality. Next time you have feelings that undermine your self-esteem, write them down. Then try to analyse the situation objectively with the help of a friend.

I'M A LABEL; YOU'RE A LABEL (LABELLING)

As with the black and white approach, labels like 'I'm a loser' or 'he's an idiot' can make life simpler. But labels take no account of change and can become self-fulfilling prophecies. Don't use them.

I SHOULD DO THIS; YOU SHOULD DO THAT (OBLIGATION)

We all have a little voice within us telling us what we *should* do. And sometimes we become the little voice telling other people what they *should* do. But doing what you allegedly 'should' isn't the same as doing what makes you happy. In future, attach more weight to happiness than to 'should'.

IF IT'S WRONG, IT MUST BE MY FAULT (WRONGLY TAKING RESPONSIBILITY).

Accepting responsibility for things that aren't your responsibility is a common error. Before accepting responsibility or blame for any situation, run through the following checklist:

- ▶ *Am I really responsible for this?*
- ▶ *Why can't the other person do this for him/herself?*
- ▶ *In what way am I so superior that only I can do this?*
- ▶ *In what way is the other person so inferior as to be incapable of doing this?*

Once you've mastered the new positive thought patterns try applying them to your past as well. You'll find that things that have been bothering you no longer seem so bad.

---

4 Goodbye to negative emotions

▶ *When you allow your anger to build up, you're actually strengthening the 'anger synapses' in your brain. In other words, you're moulding your brain for anger. Anger is exactly the opposite of what's needed for happiness.*
▶ *Negative emotions are assassins, and the person they're stalking is you. A list of the disorders related to negative emotions includes: allergies, asthma, cancers, colds and flu, depression, diabetes, headaches, heart disease, hypertension, indigestion, muscle pain and cramps, sexual problems, strokes and ulcers.*
▶ *When you feel angry with someone, protect your peace of mind and happiness with empathy – that's to say, imaginatively enter into the other person's situation. You won't feel angry any more.*
▶ *Release your stress, not by shouting, but by laughing. Laughter is a great stress buster. Learn to make yourself laugh, even if you don't feel like it. It may turn into the real thing. Laughter is actually a very powerful medicine, which can relieve pain, boost the immune system, lower blood pressure and reduce stress.*
▶ *Remember: nobody has really failed until they give up – so don't give up.*

---

5 Eating happiness

▶ *The food you eat can affect your level of happiness.*
▶ *The right foods can help create happiness by providing the raw material for 'happiness hormones' and by promoting good health.*

- The wrong foods can help create unhappiness by causing allergic reactions and poor health.
- 'Happy' foods include: alcohol in moderation; brazil nuts; coffee; chilli peppers; chocolate; complex carbohydrates in general; green leafy vegetables and legumes; garlic; oats; oysters; tea; wheatgerm.
- 'Happy' food supplements include: folic acid (folate); selenium; zinc.
- Certain foods can cause allergic reactions in susceptible individuals, resulting in low moods.

6 Inner happiness

- External happiness is something you, and others, can create. Inner happiness is different. It's more like a reservoir that can be accessed.
- Meditation is one of the ways of accessing that reservoir; it's also a way of taking control of your mind so that you can prevent unpleasant and worrying thoughts popping up uninvited.
- The lotus is the classic position for meditation, but it certainly isn't essential. You can also sit in the half-lotus, or cross-legged, or in a chair or even lie down (but be careful not to fall asleep).
- Here's a simple way of meditating for happiness:
  1 Sitting or lying down with your eyes closed, notice your breathing.
  2 Without forcing anything, gradually slow down your breathing.
  3 Make your exhalations longer than your inhalations.
  4 Empty your mind of any thoughts of past or future.
  5 Just concentrate on experiencing the present moment, which is your breath.
  6 If any thoughts push their way into your mind, just let them drift past; don't pursue them.
  7 When your breathing is slow and relaxed, notice your heartbeat.

8   *Without forcing anything, gradually try to think it slower.*

9   *Next, notice the sound of your blood in your ears.*

10 *Without forcing anything, gradually try to think it slower.*

11 *In the same way, visit any others parts of your body that you choose.*

12 *Now notice the little dots that 'illuminate' the blackness of your closed eyes.*

13 *Imagine the dots are stars and that you're floating in an immense space inside your own body.*

14 *Relax your jaw and let your mouth open into a smile.*

15 *Continue like this as long as you like.*

---

7 How to get happy-fit

▶ *Exercise is a very powerful way to make yourself happy, because it causes your body to increase production of various 'happy' chemicals, especially endorphins and phenylethylamine (PEA).*

▶ *In fact, exercise is so effective at boosting mood that in the UK the National Institute for Health and Clinical Excellence (NICE) recommends exercise together with psychotherapy as the first line of treatment for mild depression. In carefully controlled trials, exercise has performed just as well as antidepressants, but without the side effects of drugs.*

▶ *Even ten minutes of vigorous exercise is highly beneficial in terms of happiness, but more – within reason – is even better.*

▶ *It can be difficult to keep motivated, so it's important to find something you enjoy doing and that isn't expensive. Here are a few tips for keeping at it:*

  ▷ *Try to exercise at a regular time so your body comes to expect it.*

  ▷ *Exercise together with friends and jolly one another along (unless, of course, you prefer to exercise alone).*

  ▷ *Keep an exercise diary and reward yourself when you reach certain targets.*

8 Be happy being yourself

▶ *If you can't be yourself, you can't be truly happy. So take every opportunity to develop your individuality.*

▶ *Ask yourself: In what situation do I experience the maximum satisfaction of my whole being?*

▶ *You may not yet have discovered the situations that will give you the 'maximum satisfaction'. In fact, it's sometimes necessary to 'run away' to discover the answer because, quite often, the answer is only found by accident.*

▶ *Seasonal Affective Disorder (SAD) is a type of depression that can be cured by 'running away' to a better climate. If that's not possible, there are special SAD lamps that can help a lot.*

▶ *It's important to be able to say 'no', but when it comes to new experiences many people find it even harder to say 'yes'. 'No' is the option that keeps everything as it is. If you want to be happier than you are now, things have to change. That's why, sometimes, you have to say 'yes'.*

▶ *We're often told to find our 'inner child' but, in reality, children do not have the freedom to be themselves. That's why you should 'let go' your inner child and become an adult, making your own decisions and finding your own path.*

▶ *Many of the problems people suffer from in the West are avoidable. Don't inflict unnecessary problems on yourself. Ask yourself:*
  ▷ *Is this likely to make me happy at any time?*
  ▷ *Is this likely to make me unhappy at some other time?*

9 Relationships, love and happiness

▶ *You are a social animal. Connection equals happiness; loneliness equals unhappiness.*

- If you're lonely, consider getting a pet; if you're not lonely, still consider getting a pet, because pets can do many things for you.
- A pet can lower your blood pressure, reduce your level of the stress hormone cortisol, and increase your level of 'happy' chemicals. But, most of all, pets provide a model of the ideal relationship – love that is unconditional.
- Avoid the projection trap – that is, don't project your fantasies onto people; accept them as they really are, not as you'd like them to be.
- In a happy relationship, accept your partner's love the way she or he expresses it. Accept the way your partner is. Accept your partner's growth. Accept that two people are different and always will be.
- Never play 'mind games' with the people you love – be straightforward and honest, just as animals are.
- Make up your mind that if you're going to have a relationship then you're going to make it a great relationship. Nothing less.
- Do something happy together every day.

---

10 Happy sex

- Sex makes men and women equally happy.
- In one study, the couples who had the most sex were the happiest. For optimum happiness you need to have sex four times a week, or more.
- In another study, those who had had just one sexual partner in the preceding year were happier than those who had had more. In other words, for happiness be monogamous.
- In order to experience 'happy sex' to the full, both sexes need to get rid of inhibitions, introduce spirituality, cuddling and self-expression, and develop the capacity for multiple orgasms.
- In order to experience 'happy sex' to the full, you need to get rid of your inhibitions.

11 Connection equals happiness

- ▶ *Atheists can be just as spiritual as religious people.*
- ▶ *As the biologist J.B.S. Haldane once observed: 'The universe is not only queerer than we suppose, it is queerer than we can suppose.'*
- ▶ *Here are some queer things that might make you very happy:*
  - ▷ *Every atom of which you are composed came from the stars and has already been in countless other organisms.*
  - ▷ *The 'quantum' view of physics is that the properties of the parts (you) are determined by the whole (the universe).*
  - ▷ *All over the world, in every culture, people share the same 'collective unconscious'.*
- ▶ *It all amounts to one thing. You are connected. And connection equals happiness.*
- ▶ *Now build on that connection. Research shows that the happiest people are the ones who are doing something to make the world a better place. Do something generous today.*

12 Your seven-day happiness plan

For the next seven days, conduct your life in accordance with the following eight principles:

1. Start the day right: after 7–8 hours sleep get up slowly, smile and cuddle everyone in the household.
2. Be positive: prioritize the day ahead in terms of happiness.
3. No negatives: for this week you're not allowed to criticize anything or anyone (and that includes you).
4. Express yourself: be creative and let the real you come out.
5. Improve your relationships: get that oxytocin going with plenty of hugging.

6 Look after the physical: eat plenty of 'happy foods' and take plenty of 'happy exercise'.
7 Look after the spiritual: meditate.
8 Review the day: before you go to sleep, congratulate yourself on all the good things you did today.

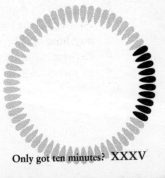

1

How happy are you?

In this chapter you will learn:
- *how happiness is something that can be learned*
- *how conscious dedication to happiness is essential*
- *how happiness is the morally right course*
- *how happiness comes from both internal and external sources.*

> *The three grand essentials to happiness in this life are something to do, something to love and something to hope for.*
>
> Joseph Addison (1672–1719), English essayist, poet and politician

Can you *really* teach yourself how to be happy? The answer is emphatically 'yes'.

You can learn how to make yourself warm and how to make yourself cold. You can learn how to make yourself hungry and how to make yourself full. You can learn all manner of things. Why should happiness be any different?

In essence, it isn't. Philosophers have long said it. Scientists have proven it. But, like so many things that have to be learned, it requires effort.

It will help if you treat being happy as a challenge, just like learning a foreign language, mastering the lotus position or climbing a mountain. It calls for single-mindedness and, quite often, the setting aside of other less important goals. To be happy you have to make happiness your priority. This is a notion that surprises many people. They think happiness should come as easily as breathing or drinking. But it doesn't.

Do you really want to be happy?

The answer would seem obvious. And the fact that you're reading this book only underlines what would appear to be common sense. Surely, everybody wants to be happy!

Well, yes, but the problem is that when it comes to making a choice between happiness and something else, people so often choose the something else. When it comes down to it, many people would choose, for example, wealth or power or 'success' over happiness. That's not to say, of course, that you can't be rich, powerful, 'successful' and happy. But there will come occasions when you're faced with a choice: happiness or wealth; happiness or power; happiness or revenge. Which will you choose then?

In a film called *City Slickers*, an old cowboy (played by the late Jack Palance) holds up a gloved finger and tells the impressionable tenderfoot Billy Crystal that the secret of happiness is just one thing. Just one. Naturally, Billy wants to know what the one thing is. Jack gives a mysterious little smile and tells him: 'That's what you've got to figure out.'

In reality, a huge number of things contribute to happiness, but if it was all to be condensed into one piece of advice, just one like Jack Palance's finger, it would have to be that to be happier than you normally are requires a conscious dedication to happiness.

So the question needs to be repeated. Do you really want to be happy?

If the answer is 'yes', this book will tell you how. It's no idle promise. Modern science has unravelled the secrets – or, rather, confirmed and explained what many philosophers have been saying for hundreds, if not thousands, of years.

So you want me to prove that I can make you happier? OK, try this: smile. Turn up the corners of your mouth, wrinkle your nose, raise your cheeks and narrow your eyes.

How does it feel? Pretty good! When you smile, even without a reason, you cause your 'happiness chemicals' to shoot up. So, in future, don't wait for a reason. Smile anyway.

Keep smiling

Just to remind you to keep smiling, you'll find boxes like this one throughout the book. They'll contain jokes relevant to the text. Only some of the jokes are funny. The jokes that aren't funny are there to test your ability to smile through adversity.

Now try these two ideas. They're a little bit more tricky:

▶ **Be grateful.** *Right now scribble down ten things you can be grateful for. Look at them and think about them. Remember that no matter how bad the situation seems, there are always things to be grateful for.*
▶ **Forgive.** *Make the decision this minute that you're going to forgive someone against whom you've been harbouring feelings of resentment. Always let go of negative emotions – when you brew poison against someone else you only end up poisoning yourself.*

These are examples of the kind of internal changes you'll need to make. How to increase your internal happiness is the subject of the first few chapters of this book. Still not happier? I don't believe it, but here are two more quick tips anyway. They're to do with external happiness, which is dealt with later in the book:

▶ **Play.** *Go and do something completely crazy immediately. Throw a paper aeroplane at the nearest person, tickle a friend,*

roll at your partner's feet like a dog and ask to have your
tummy rubbed, or put on some suitably exhilarating music,
extend your arms and 'fly' round the room. Anything. Being
playful boosts the immune system and creates optimism.
And, of course, don't forget to...

▶ **Laugh.** *If playing hasn't done it, watch a funny DVD or log
onto a humorous website. Laughter reduces stress and blood
pressure and boosts the immune system.*

*Everyone is a house with four rooms, a physical, a mental,
an emotional and a spiritual.*

*Most of us tend to live in one room most of the time, but
unless we go into every room, every day, even if only to keep
it aired, we are not a complete person.*

Indian proverb

How this book works

This book is designed for everyone who feels they're somehow
not as happy as they could be. If you're sometimes happy
but not as consistently as you'd like, or if when you're happy
you still have that nagging feeling that something isn't
quite right, that there should be more, then this book is
for you.

Unlike a lot of other books, this one tackles happiness on many
fronts. As we've seen, it aims to increase both your internal and
external happiness. It will teach you how to get rid of your
negative thoughts and emotions and replace them with positive
ones. It will encourage you to discover yourself as you are
now, to create yourself as you want to be and, above all, to be
uninhibited enough to *be* yourself. It will reveal a whole new
way of prioritizing everything in your life. It will show you how
to improve your relationships – the bedrock of happiness. It will

explain how – even for an atheist – happiness needs a spiritual component. And it will describe simple lifestyle changes that make a positive contribution to happiness.

Insight

Some people argue that you can't deliberately chase happiness because the things you *think* will make you happy seldom do in reality. According to them, happiness is an accident that either happens to you or doesn't. It's quite true that most of us are fairly bad at predicting the things that would give us the greatest happiness – a subject that's dealt with in Chapter 8. But happiness comes in two parts, 'internal' and 'external' (see *Is true happiness within or without?* below). Internal happiness will be very much within your control once you've mastered the techniques in this book. As regards external happiness, of course, there's always an element of chance, but there are also many things you can do to increase the possibility of 'getting lucky' and to reduce the chance of being 'unlucky'.

Ten things this book will do for you

1 *Increase your inner happiness.*
2 *Increase your external happiness.*
3 *Change the physical structure of your brain into that of a 'happy brain'.*
4 *Give you a more positive outlook.*
5 *Teach you how to let go of negative emotions.*
6 *Describe simple lifestyle changes that can increase happiness.*
7 *Encourage you to find happiness by being yourself.*
8 *Help you to make all your relationships happier.*
9 *Convince you that it's morally right to be happy.*
10 *Explain how to develop a happy connection with the world around you.*

Yes, I'm happy, but…

Maybe, if I asked you if you were happy, you'd answer positively. But then, after a few moments, add, 'but…'.

For most of us there's always the 'but'. Sometimes it's an identifiable 'but':

▶ *but it's difficult when my mother is so ill*
▶ *but it's difficult when I know I have to die some day*
▶ *but it's difficult when so many people are starving.*

At other times it's because something was good but not perfect:

▶ *but I'd be even happier if only I could afford such-and-such*
▶ *but I'd be even happier if I was doing this with someone I was in love with*
▶ *but I'd be even happier if it was just a little sunnier.*

For others it's much less definable:

▶ *but, I don't know, there always seems to be something lacking*
▶ *but there's always an emptiness inside*
▶ *but my soul feels alone.*

Let's deal with one of those 'buts' straight away – being happy when many others are not.

Is it morally right to be happy?

You want to be happy and yet somewhere inside a little voice is telling you it's wrong to be happy. How can you be happy, the little voice insists, when there are people who are starving?

Well, supposing I tell you that the whole point of life is to be happy? Answer this: Are you more likely to help someone else when you're feeling happy, positive and optimistic or when you're feeling miserable, irritable and low?

Undoubtedly you know the answer. And research confirms it. When you're happy you make the people around you happy. In addition, when you're happy you're far more likely to help other people than when you're feeling irritable or depressed. There's plenty of research to confirm it. So there's nothing at all wrong with wanting to be happy. On the contrary, it's the morally right course. Go ahead with a completely clear conscience.

Insight

Drivers exploding with road rage are not happy people. Robbers are not happy people. Terrorists are not happy people. When you're happy you're also far more likely to be successful in whatever you do. And, according to some beliefs, when you're in a state of happiness you're much more in tune with (whatever name you want to use) Brahma, the Great Oneness, God – because happiness is the fundamental nature of the universe.

Is true happiness within or without?

Some people say that 'true' happiness lies inside us all, if only we knew how to access it and cultivate it. Others argue that in order to be happy you need external things to be happy about – friends, romance, a comfortable home, a nice car, a well-paid job, a foreign holiday and so on.

Consider these two (seemingly very different) approaches to happiness:

- ▶ *Desiring things you haven't got makes you unhappy, so the solution is to conquer desire.*
- ▶ *Desiring things you haven't got makes you unhappy, so the solution is to get them.*

These two statements represent what might be called the 'Oriental' and 'Western' approaches. They appear to be opposites. Which is right?

As is often the case, things that appear to be opposites aren't really after all. It's more a question of degree. Of course, our Eastern philosophers have their desires, even the most ascetic: they desire to breathe, they desire to eat, they desire to drink and so on.

And if we look at Western consumers, we find that all of them have to accept that there are things they will never have: a palace, a Ferrari, a jet, a private island.

It's important to ask ourselves why we want things. Quite often, once we understand that, we discover what we really want.

There was a businessman who had made a fortune in the electronics industry. Let's call him Mr Nouveauriche. He'd bought a motorboat of which he'd been especially proud. But one day, an even richer man invited him for a drink aboard his boat and sent a launch to collect Nouveauriche. The launch turned out to be as big as Nouveauriche's new boat. From that day on, Nouveauriche was never again happy.

The point of the story is that Nouveauriche didn't want a boat so he could watch the stars at night from out at sea, or swim with dolphins, or listen to the surf breaking on remote shores. He didn't actually want a boat at all. He wanted to impress other people. His ambition was a completely false ambition. Nouveauriche was destined never to be happy. He hadn't learned, and probably never did, that the stars at night look just as good from a canoe as from the deck of the biggest yacht. He needed to cultivate in himself the appreciation of the stars that are there for all, rich and poor alike, who have eyes to see.

The truth is you need both 'internal' and 'external' happiness. Remember that your internal happiness is your baseline, the level to which you will always return. Your external happiness is a series of blips, taking you above your baseline.

It works like this. Suppose you win a large sum of money. Of course you'll be happy. Indeed, you'll probably be euphoric. But only for a couple of weeks or so. After that, you'll return to your baseline level of happiness. Don't take my word for it. Scientists have studied it, measured it and proved it. Psychologists even have a word for this process – it's called adaptation. You'll know from your own life how it works. You pass an exam, or get a raise, or buy a new car and you feel happy, but quite soon the effect wears off. You're back where you were.

The process works the other way, too. People who have suffered some terrible and permanent blow nevertheless often return to, or at least close to, their baseline happiness.

Insight

Your baseline happiness is your foundation. And unless you can arrange your life so that wonderful things are constantly happening to you, it's the level of happiness you'll enjoy most of the time. Unfortunately, your baseline has a lot to do with genetics (see box below). Raising the baseline means tinkering with the most fundamental aspects of the way you look at life. It can be done, but you're going to have to be ready to reappraise a lot of your ideas.

YOUR HAPPINESS AND YOUR GENES

David Lykken, emeritus psychology professor at the University of Minnesota, has studied hundreds of identical twins, including those who were separated shortly after birth. His conclusion is that happiness is 'at least 50 per cent inherited'.

It seems there are genes related to happiness as well as genes related to negative thinking and anxiety. In other words, some people are simply born happier than others.

Other scientists have put the percentage due to heredity as low as 30 per cent or as high as 70 per cent. But even the scientists who put the genetic factor at the top end, still concede that how happy you feel right now (or any time) is about half due to the circumstances. In other words, even someone born with a low genetic tendency to be happy can be pretty happy if something good happens. So one of the answers is to make sure nice things keep happening – and we'll be looking at that later in the book.

In any event, your genes don't tie you to a specific level of happiness. Rather, they seem to create a tendency towards a certain range of happiness. This book will teach you how to stay at the top of your range.

But there's another difference in the brains of people who are generally happy and those who are generally unhappy. Richard Davidson, a neuropsychologist at the University of Wisconsin-Madison, has discovered that people in whom the left side of the prefrontal cortex dominates are self-confident, optimistic and happy, while those in whom the right side dominates tend to be suspicious, pessimistic and unhappy.

About a third of people are thought to be left dominant, a third neutral and a third right dominant. In the short term, the side that dominates doesn't change with circumstances but is a part of your personality. But in the long term, you can learn to switch from right-side to left-side dominance.

Davidson confirmed this by testing ten-year-olds whom he'd also studied as babies and found that, in many cases, the dominant side had changed.

But perhaps the strongest evidence came from a man whom Davidson found to have the greatest left-side activity he'd encountered in 20 years. The man was a Tibetan monk who had meditated for more than 10,000 hours. (To find out how meditation can make you happier see Chapter 6.)

(To find out how meditation can make you happier see Chapter 6.)

Try this

A lot of books on happiness start by posing the question: 'What is happiness?'

As far as this book is concerned, if you feel happy you are happy. If you feel extremely happy, you are extremely happy. But, here's an interesting thing. If you feel fed up or even depressed you may not be as consistently low as you think you are. When depressed people are asked to keep a 'happiness diary' – keeping a note of every time they feel happy and why – they quite often fill a page a day.

So this is your first exercise. Start a 'happiness diary' today and, as you progress through this book, trying out the various ideas, make a note of how well they work for you.

Insight

Write down all the times you feel happy and give the reason – if you can work it out. You're almost certainly in for a big surprise. In fact, I guarantee you'll discover things about your own happiness that will astonish you.

Emma's story

I was driving down a country lane. It was warm and sunny and I had the windows open. The verges on both sides were covered with wild flowers. I slowed right down so I could see them better and I suddenly realized, to my astonishment, that I was completely and utterly happy. It was almost frightening. Normally I don't even like driving. It stresses me. So I never would have predicted that I could be so happy at that moment. I stopped the car, got out and started looking – really looking – at the flowers.

I was completely overcome. Even now I can't explain it.

CASE STUDY

How happy are you?

Since I'm claiming I can make you happier, we'll need some tangible proof. Here are some self-tests. Fill them in now. When you finish the book do the tests again and see how much higher on the 'happiness scale' you score.

Throughout the book you'll also find a number of practical exercises. You'll get a lot more out of the book if you complete them. In Chapter 1, for example, I advised you to make a list of all the things you should be grateful for. I hope you didn't say to yourself, 'OK, I've got the idea', and then leave it at that. Grasping the idea is not enough. You still need to complete the exercise to make the maximum progress.

So let's see what we're up against.

1 **How do you feel?**

    a Extremely depressed
    b Quite depressed
    c Unhappy
    d Neutral
    e Happy
    f Extremely happy
    g Ecstatic

2 **With what frequency do you think you experience happy feelings?**

    a Hardly ever
    b Occasionally
    c A bit less than half the time
    d About half the time
    e A bit more than half the time
    f Most of the time
    g Pretty much all the time

3 **What do you think your baseline happiness level is (the level you're at when nothing unusually good or bad has happened)?**

   a Extremely depressed
   b Quite depressed
   c Unhappy
   d Neutral
   e Happy
   f Extremely happy
   g Ecstatic

4 **Here we're taking a look at your willingness to be happy. Say whether you a) strongly agree, b) slightly agree, c) neither agree nor disagree, d) slightly disagree, e) strongly disagree.**

   i   I can't really be happy when other people are starving.
   ii I can't really be happy when so many animals face extinction.
   iii I can't really be happy when global warming threatens the planet.
   iv Even if you're rich you should still work and be useful.
   v   Rich people are often very unhappy.
   vi A life of hedonism is futile.
   vii You just can't do whatever you want.
   viii There's a lot more to life than just having a good time.
   ix I'm worried I won't know what to do when I retire.
   x   Sex should be within marriage.
   xi It's wrong to have sex for fun.
   xii Sexually transmitted diseases are a punishment for immoral behaviour.
   xiii You've got to learn to stick at things and not keep chopping and changing.
   xiv It's no good trying to run away from things because you'll find problems wherever you go.
   xv Good people will get their reward in the next life.

5 **How would you assess the effort you make to be happy?**

   a   I try to find happiness in everything.
   b   I aim to do at least one happy thing every day.
   c   I generally leave happiness to chance.

6 **How often do you get your heart rate up for at least 20 minutes?**

   a   Hardly ever
   b   Now and then
   c   Once a week
   d   Three times a week
   e   Most days

7 **How would you assess your eating habits?**

   a   I eat anything that tastes nice and I'm overweight.
   b   I eat anything that tastes nice but I'm the correct weight.
   c   I choose my foods on the basis of how healthy they are but I'm overweight.
   d   I choose my foods on the basis of how healthy they are and I'm the correct weight.

8 **What are your spiritual beliefs?**

   a   I don't have any spiritual feelings at all.
   b   I feel a bit spiritual.
   c   I feel very spiritual.

9 **How would you assess your relationship, if you have one?**

   We are:

   a   deeply in love and inseparable.
   b   deeply in love but quite independent of one another.

c in love, but it's not really a romance like the movies.
d fond of one another but a bit bored.
e unhappy together.
f at one another's throats.

10 How would you assess your sex life?

a I have a partner and our sex life together is incredibly good.
b I have a partner and our sex life together is quite good.
c I have a partner and our sex life together is satisfactory.
d I have a partner and our sex life together is not very good.
e I have a partner and our sex life together is poor.
f I have a partner and our sex life together is bad.
g I don't have a regular partner but my sex life is pretty good.
h I don't have a regular partner so I don't have sex very often.
i I have no sex life at all.

11 How would you assess your social life?

a I'm very close to family and/or friends; there's always someone I can depend on.
b I see family and/or friends quite often but there's no one I feel very close to.
c I have family and/or friends I see occasionally.
d I feel a great gulf between myself and everybody else.

12 How would you assess your job, if you have one?

a I find it very rewarding and look forward to it.
b I enjoy it some of the time.
c I need the money and I don't mind the job.
d I need the money but I'm not very happy at work.
e I need the money but I hate the job.
f I'm unemployed.

13 How would you assess your freedom to be yourself?

    a I express myself freely and behave exactly as I want.
    b I express myself fairly freely and behave more or less as I want.
    c I can occasionally express myself freely and occasionally behave as I want.
    d I can't ever express myself freely or behave as I want.

14 Which of the following most closely represents your view?

    a I like everything to correspond perfectly with the way I imagine it should be.
    b I imagine how things might be but I'm quite ready for them to be different.
    c I don't have preconceived ideas; I always find something to be happy about.

15 How do you regard the future?

    a I feel optimistic because I always make sure I have things to look forward to.
    b I don't look forward with any great sense of anticipation, but I'm not worried either.
    c I feel apprehensive about the future.

16 How would you assess your self-esteem?

    a I've been very fortunate and have done extremely well in life.
    b I've done pretty well but with a few regrets.
    c I know there are plenty of people who have done a lot better than me, but there are also plenty who have done a lot worse.
    d There are plenty of ways in which I could improve and I'm working on that, but I'm satisfied with the way things are going.
    e I feel I haven't achieved much in my life so far, but there's still time.

f I feel I haven't achieved much in my life, but it doesn't bother me.

g I feel I haven't achieved much in my life and therefore I'm a failure.

17 How would you assess your charitable feelings?

a I try hard to make the world a better place.

b I try hard to help everyone I know.

c I try hard to help those who are close to me.

d I may not have done much good, but I don't think I've done any harm to anybody or anything either.

e I just let the world get on as it wants and don't get involved.

f I try to get what I want and to hell with anyone or anything that gets in my way.

18 How would you assess your self-knowledge?

a I think my opinion of myself is accurate because it more or less accords with that of other people.

b Other people think I have an overly high opinion of myself, but they're probably jealous.

c Other people tell me I have too low an opinion of myself.

19 How would you assess your self-love?

a I love everything about myself.

b I'm happy as I am and I accept my imperfections.

c I like myself quite a bit but I'm working on ways in which I can improve.

d I hate everything about myself.

20 This final section assesses the vulnerability of your happiness. Read the following statements and then say whether you a) strongly agree, b) slightly agree, c) neither agree nor disagree, d) slightly disagree, e) strongly disagree.

i My feelings of self-worth greatly depend on other people's opinions of me.

ii I could never be happy without loving someone and that person loving me.

iii It's essential to excel at something and have other people admire you for it.

iv If you're not a perfectionist, you just won't get on in life.

v If I see that something is right then, obviously, I get angry if other people want to do it differently.

vi I have a responsibility for the happiness and wellbeing of people close to me.

vii My moods are created by the things that happen to me.

YOUR SCORE

Questions 1–3. These are self-explanatory. Score 0 for each a), 100 for each b), 200 for each c), 300 for each d), 400 for each e), 500 for each f) and 600 for each g).

	Score now	Score after reading the book
Q1	....	....
Q2	....	....
Q3	....	....

Question 4. Score 0 for an a), 1 for a b), 2 for a c), 3 for a d) and 4 for an e).

	Score now	Score after reading the book
Q4	....	....

Interpretation:

0–20. You're never going to allow yourself to be happy. But your high moral tone is based on a misapprehension. Your being unhappy doesn't help anybody and, indeed, makes some people's lives worse. It's not immoral to be happy. Read (or re-read) this book and try hard to change your attitudes.

21–40. You're quite often able to be happy but your sense of wellbeing is frequently destroyed by bad news of various kinds.

Of course you should empathize with others but, remember, you being unhappy doesn't help anybody.

41–60. Your happiness is seldom spoiled by the problems other people have. It doesn't mean you don't care. On the contrary, you may care very much – but you've learned that you can help without having to be made unhappy yourself.

Question 5. Score 60 for an a), 30 for a b) and 0 for a c).

	Score now	Score after reading the book
Q5	....	....

Interpretation:

60. You have the right attitude in trying to find happiness in everything you do.

30. You're doing a good thing by insisting on at least one happy event in a day, but you're not maximizing your potential happiness. And you're leaving yourself vulnerable if the big thing in your day doesn't work out.

0. Don't leave something as important as happiness to chance.

Question 6. Score 0 for an a), 10 for a b), 20 for a c), 40 for a d) and 60 for an e).

	Score now	Score after reading the book
Q6	....	....

Interpretation:

Numerous studies have shown beyond any doubt that there's a direct link between exercise and not only health but happiness, too. You should be aiming for 20 minutes of moderate exercise three to five days a week. Exercise literally generates the chemicals that make us feel happy – you'll find full details in Chapter 7.

Question 7. Score 0 for an a), 10 for a b), 30 for a c) and 60 for a d).

	Score now	Score after reading the book
Q7	....	....

Interpretation:

Healthy eating promotes happiness in various ways, not least because it provides the raw materials from which 'happiness chemicals' are made. At the same time, it prevents damage to parts of the body that are essential to happiness – you'll find full details in Chapter 5.

Question 8. Score 0 for an a), 20 for a b) and 60 for a c).

	Score now	Score after reading the book
Q8	....	....

Interpretation:

If you don't have any spiritual beliefs there's always going to be a little void inside you that you'll never fill, no matter how many things you do to make yourself happy. You'll find full details in Chapter 11.

Question 9. Score 60 for an a), 50 for a b), 30 for a c), 20 for a d), 10 for an e) and 0 for an f).

	Score now	Score after reading the book
Q9	....	....

Interpretation:

Close relationships are fundamental to happiness. Married people (or those in enduring partnerships) not only live longer but they're generally more content than people who are single, widowed or divorced. You'll find full details in Chapter 9.

Question 10. Score 60 for an a), 50 for a b), 40 for a c), 20 for a d), 10 for an e), 0 for an f), 30 for a g), 10 for an h) and 0 for an i).

	Score now	Score after reading the book
Q10	....	....

Interpretation:

According to some psychologists there's a formula for judging the happiness of any relationship – frequency of sex minus frequency of rows. And a good relationship, as already noted, is vitally important to happiness. But there's more to it than that. Sex generates chemicals that make us feel good. You'll find full details in Chapter 10.

Question 11. Score 60 for an a), 40 for a b), 20 for a c) and 0 for a d).

	Score now	Score after reading the book
Q11	....	....

Interpretation:

Family and friends sustain us when the going gets tough and are a source of fun and laughter the rest of the time. You'll find full details in Chapter 9.

Question 12. Score 60 for an a), 40 for a b), 30 for a c), 20 for a d), 10 for an e) and 0 for an f).

	Score now	Score after reading the book
Q12	....	....

Interpretation:

You're probably going to spend something like a third of your adult waking hours at work. So job satisfaction is extremely important on that basis alone. But, in addition, work possibly gives such meaning to your life that you'd do it even if you didn't need the money. You'll find full details in Chapter 8.

Question 13. Score 60 for an a), 40 for a b), 20 for a c) and 0 for a d).

	Score now	Score after reading the book
Q13	....	....

Interpretation:

It's vital that you should feel free to develop as the person you truly are. You'll never be happy if you're constrained either by your own inhibitions or by the need to conform with what others, wrongly, expect of you. You'll find full details in Chapter 8.

Question 14. Score 0 for an a), 30 for a b) and 60 for a c).

	Score now	Score after reading the book
Q14	....	....

Interpretation:

Struggling to create perfect scenarios is almost certain to fail. It means you're trying to impose your needs on other people and the world. Unfortunately, things are always going to go wrong and you're always going to be disappointed. You'll find full details in Chapter 3.

Question 15. Score 60 for an a), 30 for a b) and 0 for a c).

	Score now	Score after reading the book
Q15	....	....

Interpretation:

It's essential to have a sense of moving forward in life, to believe that tomorrow will be at least as good as today, if not better, and that progress is being made. You'll find full details in Chapter 8.

Question 16. Score 60 for an a), 50 for a b), 40 for a c), 40 for a d), 30 for an e), 40 for an f) add 0 for a g).

	Score now	Score after reading the book
Q16	....	....

Interpretation:

Self-esteem is very important for happiness. Conversely, low self-esteem is linked with depression. For most people, self-esteem is related to achievements. But if you can learn to see your self-worth in other aspects of your life, you'll be less vulnerable. You'll find full details in Chapter 3.

Question 17. Score 60 for an a), 60 for a b), 50 for a c), 30 for a d), 20 for an e) and 0 for an f).

	Score now	Score after reading the book
Q17	....	....

Interpretation:

Surveys show that people who go out of their way to help others feel happier than other people. You'll find full details in Chapter 11.

Question 18. Score 60 for an a), 30 for a b) and 0 for a c).

	Score now	Score after reading the book
Q18	....	....

Interpretation:

Well-balanced people see themselves very much as others see them.

Question 19. Score 60 for an a), 60 for a b), 40 for a c) and 0 for a d).

	Score now	Score after reading the book
Q19	....	....

Interpretation:

If you're not fairly happy with yourself then you're just not going to be happy at all. It's that simple. You'll find full details in Chapter 8.

Question 20. Score 0 for each a), 2 for each b), 4 for each c), 6 for each d), 8 for each e) and 10 for each f).

	Score now	Score after reading the book
Q20	....	....

0–20. Your happiness is extremely vulnerable to the things life throws at you. You need to work on this, otherwise whatever happiness you manage to develop will always be built on a shaky foundation.

21–45. Like most people you can rise above a certain amount of misfortune, but greater happiness depends on you developing a more resilient baseline.

46–70. Lucky you. You can still be happy in the face of all manner of setbacks. But don't be complacent; keep working on it.

Interpretation:

A low score doesn't automatically mean you'll be unhappy – as long as nothing goes wrong. But the more vulnerable you are (low score) the more easily your happiness will be destroyed when there's a problem. You'll find full details in Chapter 3.

10 THINGS TO REMEMBER

1 *You can teach yourself to be happy.*

2 *If there's one single key to happiness, it's conscious dedication to happiness.*

3 *Happiness is the point of life.*

4 *Happy people are more likely to help others, so it's morally right to be happy.*

5 *You need both 'internal' and 'external' sources of happiness.*

6 *Everyone has a baseline level of happiness, which can be raised.*

7 *Although genes are partially responsible for happiness, you can learn how to stay near the top of that genetic range and to maximize the part of happiness that isn't genetically determined.*

8 *You can learn to switch from right-side to left-side dominance in the prefrontal cortex, and be happier.*

9 *Keep a 'happiness diary' – you'll be amazed at the results.*

10 *Complete the above tests once again after reading this book.*

Keep smiling

Time is the best teacher, although it eventually kills the students.

2

Building a happy brain

In this chapter you will learn:
- *how your brain can be physically remodelled as a 'happy brain'*
- *how your thoughts affect your mood*
- *how negative thoughts and emotions can literally poison you*
- *how your basic outlook, formed in infancy, can be changed.*

> *We can throw stones, complain about them, stumble on them, climb over them, or build with them.*
>
> William Arthur Ward (1921–94), American author

When you're happy you learn faster – it's a scientific fact. So while you're reading, keep smiling.

One of the most important secrets of happiness is that your brain is 'plastic'. In other words, it can be moulded – in effect, in the same way as a muscle. And not just when you're an infant. All through your life your brain has the capacity for physical change, so that's reassuring as it's never too late. Only a very few functions are irrevocably set in childhood. You have it in your power to mould your own brain and make it a happy brain.

How does it work? Well, neurologists have captured the essence of it with this saying: 'Cells that fire together wire together.' It's one of the answers to the riddle of how the brain functions.

When two things happen at once, such as seeing the sun and feeling a delicious warmth on your skin, so two sets of neurons are set off in your brain and a connection, known as a synapse, is made between them. You've now learned that sunshine means pleasure. And forever more, when you see the sun, you'll feel happy. What's more, each time you feel the pleasure, the synapse will be strengthened. This is called Hebbian Learning, after the Canadian psychologist Donald Hebb who, as far back as 1949, proposed that single neurons were responsible for the learning process.

In other words, learning is simply wiring in new connections between some of the 100 billion neurons you have in your brain. The more something is repeated, the more lasting the wiring becomes. That's why, when you repeat things over and over, you can remember them more easily. And the growth of this wiring has even been observed using something called a two-photon fluorescence microscope, so it's not a hypothesis, it's reality. When a lot of new wiring is added in a particular area of the brain it actually becomes physically larger. Some regions can grow incredibly quickly – in just a few hours – but others take weeks or even years.

When you rewire your brain for happiness you're working at the most profound level by elevating your baseline. In other words, although life's problems and tragedies may sometimes knock you down, and although occasional good fortune may sometimes fly you to the moon, this is the base level to which you'll always return.

Insight

If you're fairly typical, you can start increasing your baseline level of happiness in just a few days. But if you've been depressed for a while, then it's going to take longer. That's because the physical structure of your brain has changed to that of a 'depressed brain'. Be ready for that and don't be put off. You can do it. You're just going to need a little more patience than some other people.

One of the ways of working at this deep level is through your thoughts. The concept is profound and yet very simple. If you deliberately think happy thoughts you'll not only feel happier, but the chemicals that are linked to your thoughts will bring about physical changes in your brain.

Is happiness a madness?

Dr Richard Bentall, a psychologist at Liverpool University, has suggested that happiness should be considered pathological (related to or caused by disease) because it's:

- ▶ associated with irrational thinking
- ▶ caused by a disturbance of the central nervous system
- ▶ a frequent side effect of epileptic fits.

If he's right, you're very soon going to be completely mad!

Retraining your mind

Let's say your boss tells you you're going to get an unexpected and quite substantial Christmas bonus. You're thrilled. A little later one of your colleagues tells you the size of her Christmas bonus and it's double yours. Now how do you feel?

And yet your circumstances haven't changed. The same bonus that made you happy a couple of hours ago now makes you unhappy.

What has changed is your mental attitude. You were content with the sum you were getting. Now you're not.

This is an illustration of the principle that your happiness has a lot to do with your way of looking at things.

Your living is determined not so much by what life brings to you as by the attitude you bring to life; not so much by what happens to you as by the way your mind looks at what happens.

John Homer Miller (1722–91), American author

One of the keys to more happiness, then, is to adopt a way of thinking that leads to happiness.

In our little scenario, you could storm into the boss's office and demand that you also be given a larger bonus. You might get it. Then again, you might not. Alternatively, you could continue to be miserable with the bonus you have. But if happiness is your aim, then all you really have to do is be grateful for what you got.

This idea that happiness comes from you controlling your own mind (rather than the outside world) has long been a teaching of Oriental philosophy. But, relatively recently, it has also become a teaching of modern psychology. In the 1960s, Dr Aaron Beck at the University of Pennsylvania School of Medicine began codifying the different kinds of thinking that lead to happiness and unhappiness. As a result, he developed a system for treating depression and various other mental problems, which he called 'cognitive therapy'.

Let's say you get the sack. These are two possible responses:

1 *I'm a failure; I'll never get another job now.*
2 *I was never really happy there and that was part of the problem; I'll learn from this, move ahead and get a job I really like.*

Obviously, if you were to respond as in the first example, you'd be talking yourself into a depression and building a depressed brain. But if you were to respond as in the second example, you'd be much happier – and, incidentally, far more likely to get another job.

Change your surname

Researchers have discovered that surnames affect
personality. If yours begins with one of the first letters of
the alphabet you're likely to be happier and more confident
than if it begins with one of the last letters. Apparently, it's
all to do with whether you're one of the first or one of the
last to be dealt with whenever there's a queue. So change
your name to Aardvark and you should be very happy.

This more positive way of looking at the world is the essence
of cognitive therapy (or cognitive behavioural therapy). It's a
rather highfalutin title to describe something that, in fact,
we all use on ourselves every day. Whenever we try to cajole
ourselves into attempting something difficult ('I can do this'),
or whenever we try to raise our own spirits ('It's not so bad'),
or whenever we try to counter a criticism ('He doesn't know
what he's talking about'), we're using cognitive therapy (CT).
In other words, we're trying to make ourselves feel better by
changing the way we think.

Insight

Some people object to CT on the grounds that it implies that
problems aren't real but are 'all in the mind'. That's a
misunderstanding of CT. Of course CT recognizes that the
situation is real. The facts are the facts, but you may be
perceiving them in a distorted way and reacting accordingly.

Ten thoughts that can make you unhappy

When you put CT together with philosophy from ancient
traditions, such as Taoism and Buddhism, you see a lot of

similarities and you end up with a list that looks something like this:

1 *Theirs is better. (comparing)*
2 *I want more... and more. (greed)*
3 *If it's not black, it must be white. (all-or-nothing)*
4 *If it's not perfect, it's no good. (perfectionism)*
5 *Why is this always happening to me? (exaggeration)*
6 *I'm not going to like this. (jumping to negative conclusions)*
7 *I feel it, so it must be true. (emotional reasoning)*
8 *I'm a label; you're a label. (labelling)*
9 *I should do this; you should do that. (obligation)*
10 *If it's wrong, it must be my fault. (wrongly taking responsibility)*

Now let's take a look at these thoughts in detail.

THEIRS IS BETTER

We've all heard of the Joneses and we're all very used to the concept of trying to keep up with them. So much so that in fact we probably don't even question it. The Christmas bonus scenario reveals that comparing in this way *can* be a source of unhappiness. But do you really want your life dictated by the Joneses? Have you ever stopped to ask if what the Joneses want is what you want, too? It may not be.

It also has to do with 'bestliness' – a constant human preoccupation. Which is the *best* car? Who is the *best* writer? Where is the *best* restaurant? Again, we've been conditioned to think this way. But wouldn't it make more sense to ask: Does this make me happy? The 'best' may not.

I WANT MORE... AND MORE

Wanting more seems to be perfectly normal. After all, isn't that progress? The problem is that although greed can sometimes be satisfied in the short term, it never can be in the long term. Nothing is ever enough, which is why our materialistic, consumer society, for all its successes, produces such a surprising amount of unhappiness. If happiness is your goal, you need a different way of looking at things.

IF IT'S NOT BLACK, IT MUST BE WHITE

Some people like their lives to be simple, and nothing simplifies life as much as this mindset. Those who say, 'Either you're for me or you're against me' have the all-or-nothing outlook. Black-and-whiters don't have many friends and their close relationships are difficult: 'If you won't do that you obviously don't love me.' Even more unhappiness comes when it's turned inwards: 'I'm not first so therefore I'm a loser.'

IF IT'S NOT PERFECT, IT'S NO GOOD

Perfectionists aren't happy unless everything is just the way they want it to be. Which means they're never happy. Striving for a high standard is one thing; perfectionism is something completely different. You'll not only be happier, you'll also be much more productive turning out competent work than chasing the elusive perfection.

WHY IS THIS ALWAYS HAPPENING TO ME?

But does it always happen to you? Of course not. You're exaggerating. Don't keep focusing on the few things that go wrong and building up their importance. Instead, keep your mind on the many things that go right. Don't magnify the negative and don't minimize the positive.

Some people walk in the rain. Others just get wet.
Roger Miller (1936–92), American songwriter

I'M NOT GOING TO LIKE THIS

Some people don't even wait for the negative to arrive before they start torturing themselves. They see three people whispering in a corner and are immediately convinced that nasty things are being said about them. They jump to negative conclusions. Why assume the worst? That certainly isn't the way to happiness. Try assuming the best instead.

I FEEL IT, SO IT MUST BE TRUE

You feel like a failure, so therefore you must be a failure. This style of emotional reasoning is a common feature of low moods and depression. You allow your feelings to overwhelm you and cloud your judgement. You feel helpless in the face of a problem and conclude that there is no solution.

I'M A LABEL; YOU'RE A LABEL

Labelling yourself and others is a trap. As soon as you give yourself a label ('I'm a failure'), you talk yourself into being one. As soon as you label others ('he's a moron'), you prevent yourself from being able to see the whole human being. You can't judge yourself or others on the basis of one event, such as a failed exam.

I SHOULD DO THIS; YOU SHOULD DO THAT

Somewhere inside is a little voice telling you what you should do. You should clean the spare room. You should cut the grass. You think there's some kind of obligation. The same little voice also wants to boss other people around: he should take more care of his appearance; she should get a better job. When you don't do what you should, you feel guilt; when other people don't do what they should, you feel resentment (emotions that are dealt with in Chapter 4).

IF IT'S WRONG, IT MUST BE MY FAULT

Taking responsibility for your own decisions and mistakes is a positive character trait. Wrongly taking responsibility for what everybody else does is not. When your elderly father insists on driving, when your partner wears clothes you find embarrassing or when your son fails to do his homework, these things are their responsibility, not yours.

Not everybody would agree that all of the above ways of thinking are 'wrong'. But it really doesn't matter one way or the other. What does matter is that they cause unhappiness. And if you want to be happy (remember, you said you did), then you don't want to follow those lines of thought.

> ### Try this
> **Now that you know what the ten unhappy ways of thinking are, how many do you agree with?** That's to say, do you, for example, think it's a good idea to aim for perfection? Do you see greed as a positive – the motor behind improved living standards – or as a negative that causes misery? Write down your feelings now and see if you still hold them when you've finished this book.

Ten harmful emotions

In addition to the ten unhappy ways of thinking, there are also at least ten harmful emotions. They are feelings that literally poison our minds in the same way that cyanide would poison our bodies. We take great care to avoid poisonous substances. We need to exercise the same care in keeping negative emotions away from our minds. These negative emotions include:

1 *anger*
2 *blame*
3 *cynicism*
4 *hate*
5 *hostility*
6 *revenge*
7 *jealousy*
8 *resentment*
9 *suspicion*
10 *indifference*.

Why are we negative?

It's worth asking why you or anybody else should want to look at
things in a negative way. After all, if looking for the positive leads
to happiness, and if looking for the negative leads to everything
bad, then only a fool would look for the negative. And yet so many
people do.

According to many psychiatrists and psychologists, infants very
quickly develop into one of four types, rather entertainingly
expressed like this:

1 *I'm all right and you're all right.*
2 *I'm all right but you're not all right.*
3 *I'm not all right but you're all right.*
4 *I'm not all right and you're not all right.*

You can probably grasp right away that the first of these is most
likely to lead to happiness. The second will lead to occasional
happiness. The third and fourth are recipes for unhappiness.

According to this theory, once the thought pattern has developed,
so it will continue for the rest of your life, unless you make a
conscious effort to change. And this is the key point. A person
will interpret everything that happens in the world in one of these

four ways. In other words, four different people (one from each category) can have the identical experience and yet each will find in it the 'proof' that their own philosophy is the right one.

Here's a little test to see which category you are. Suppose the economy of the country has got into serious difficulties and a leading politician has come on the television to explain what has happened. Which of the following do you say?

1 *The government has done a pretty good job up to now and I'm sure he's as disappointed as we all are. It will come right again.*
2 *You idiot! A bunch of monkeys would make a better job of running the country.*
3 *These things are too complicated for me but I'm sure he's clever enough to solve the problem.*
4 *Why does everything have to go wrong for me? What a lousy world!*

These four kinds of response correspond to the four types of personality.

If you're type 1, you're lucky. You're happy. Your self-worth doesn't rely on seeing other people as inferior. You can empathize freely without being judgmental. You don't see the world as hostile. But this is the hardest of the four positions to maintain consistently.

If you're type 2, you may have had parents who tended to view the world with a certain hostility. They and you (and other close family members) were OK (in fact, far more than OK), but everyone else was incompetent and potentially dangerous. You relish seeing everyone else as 'not OK' because in order to maintain your own sense of superiority, and therefore your self-worth, you need other people to be failures. You may not be very happy but, on the other hand, you're unlikely to become depressed.

If you're type 3, you may have had parents who were often 'disappointed' in you and critical. You feel that you're to blame when things go wrong. You feel that other people are more successful and happy than you are. Unfortunately, you may indulge in behaviour that will have the effect of confirming your belief, such as drinking heavily. You're liable to become depressed.

If you're type 4, you're often depressed. You derive little pleasure from anything. There seems to be no way out.

If you recognize yourself as type 2, 3 or 4 don't worry. This book will teach you how to transform yourself into type 1. It can be done.

Getting rid of the negative

You may object that mindsets such as perfectionism and driving ambition are aspects of your personality, along with emotions such as anger and jealousy. You may feel that they're natural and can't be eradicated in you or any other human being. And that if they were to be eradicated in you then you just wouldn't be 'you' any more.

Well, lots of things are unnatural. It's not 'natural', for example, to be able to read this book, nor to cut your fingernails and, as Dr Bentall has suggested, it may not even be 'natural' to be happy very often. But that's what we're aiming for. So let's not worry about what's 'natural' and what isn't.

As regards your personality, that's a different issue. It's certainly true that if you're to become happier, then your personality is going to change. Indeed, in a sense, yes, you won't be 'you' any more. You'll be different. Be ready for that if you want to be happier. But who knows which is the 'real' you anyway? Maybe it's the happy version.

In the next chapter you'll learn how to tackle the poisons.

It is not the strongest of the species that survive, nor the most intelligent, but the one most responsive to change.

Charles Darwin (1809–82), English scientist

10 THINGS TO REMEMBER

1 Your brain is plastic, which means it can be rebuilt as a 'happy brain'.

2 The process of physically changing the brain through new ideas is known as Hebbian Learning.

3 The best way to change your brain is to change your thoughts.

4 Cognitive therapy (CT) is a highly effective way of changing your thought patterns.

5 There are (at least) ten unhappy ways of thinking.

6 There are (at least) ten harmful emotions.

7 The happiest outlook is, 'I'm all right and you're all right.'

8 Negative attitudes can be set in infancy and can only be changed by a deliberate effort.

9 Being frequently happy may not be a natural state, which means you may have to employ 'unnatural' measures to attain it.

10 Becoming happier means changing your personality – be ready for that.

HOW HAPPY ARE YOU NOW?

When somebody new arrives at work, or when you're introduced to someone at a party, which of the following most closely reflects your usual reaction?

a *Here's a great opportunity to make another friend.*
b *Here's someone who's probably going to be a nuisance.*
c *Here's someone who probably won't like me.*

If you answered (a) then you obviously have the 'I'm all right and you're all right' mentality that's a recipe for happiness. Move on to Chapter 3. If you answered (b) or (c) you obviously have some work to do in this area. Ask yourself why other people aren't 'all right' or why, if it's the case, you're not 'all right'. Reflect that to everyone else on the planet *you* are another person. Reread this chapter before moving on to Chapter 3, where I'll be looking at some of the negative feelings you can have about other people and yourself, and how you can overcome them.

Keep smiling

The fact that no one understands you doesn't mean you're an artist.

3

Think yourself happy

In this chapter you will learn:
- *how thinking happy thoughts will make you happy*
- *how thinking negative thoughts will make you unhappy*
- *how you can rewrite your past.*

> *There has been much tragedy in my life; at least half of it actually happened.*
>
> Mark Twain (1835–1910), American writer

You are what you think. Think exclusively happy thoughts and you'll become a profoundly happy person. On the other hand, think unhappy thoughts and the reverse will be the case.

'Too simplistic!' I hear you say. 'How can I have happy thoughts when something bad is happening?'

The answer is that, like Mark Twain, many of us tend to have thoughts that are far more negative than the reality demands. In fact, he was only right in principle as he is wrong on proportion: most of our negative thoughts are unwarranted.

In Chapter 2 I described some of those negative ways of looking at the world. In this chapter I'm going to tell you how to overcome them. Remember, it's not just a question of feeling better about a particular situation. By changing the way you think you're actually going to rebuild your brain as a 'happy brain'.

Theirs is better

Let me ask you this. Are you happier when you listen to music on an MP3 player than when you listen to the same music on a CD player? And did the music on the CD player make you happier than listening to it on a tape cassette? And did the cassette make you happier than listening at 33 1/3 rpm? Of course not; it's the music that counts.

In the same way, if you drive to meet friends for coffee, will you enjoy their company more because your transport is a Ferrari as opposed to an old banger? Of course not; it's the company that counts.

So often we lose sight of the function of the products we buy. Instead we become obsessed with impressing other people. Quite often the comparisons are false anyway.

Insight

In some ways, advertising is among the greatest curses of our era. We're encouraged to compare our lifestyles and possessions with the richest people on the planet. We're urged to be dissatisfied unless we have the very latest products, as they do. We're told that only 'the best' will do for us. In short, we're made miserable.

Try this

1 *For the next week:*

▶ *Don't look at any advertising.*
▶ *Don't go window-shopping.*
▶ *Don't read any magazines depicting celebrities.*

2 *Save up until you can afford to buy four bottles of red wine in different price categories. Wrap the bottles in newspaper,*

invite some friends around and ask them in a 'blind tasting' to say which wine they prefer. It's unlikely to be the most expensive.

3 *If you insist on comparing, then instead of comparing with people who are wealthier than you, start comparing with people who are poorer than you. You'll be much more content – it's been proven in various experiments.*

4 *If you live in the UK, compare with:*

▶ *the million households that are in debt to door-to-door moneylenders*
▶ *the 10.5 million people who can't afford to save, insure their house contents or spend even small amounts on themselves.*

5 *If you live in the USA compare with:*

▶ *the 15.6 million Americans who live in extreme poverty*
▶ *the 37 million Americans who live below the official poverty line.*

6 *If you're in one of those categories, then compare with:*

▶ *the 25,000 people who die every day from hunger or hunger-related problems*
▶ *the 640 million children who don't have adequate shelter*
▶ *the 3 billion people who live on less than £1 (approx. US$1.50) a day.*

7 *Draw up a little table in which you can enter some of the possessions which, as a result of comparing, you feel dissatisfied with. Then re-examine them from the perspective of whether or not they actually perform their function.*

The table might look something like this:

Item	Intended function	Does it perform its function?	Would a new one function better?
CD player	playing music	yes	no, because what counts is the music
TV	watching TV	yes	no, because what counts are the programmes
car	transport	yes	no, because what counts is where I go

Problem: If I don't compare I won't get the best or be the best

You're suffering from 'bestliness'. How quickly you've forgotten that you wanted to be happy. That's what you said, anyway. So which is it? Do you want the best gadget or happiness? If you want to be happy, don't compare.

I want more... and more

If you're the kind of person who always has to have more and more then, by definition, you'll never be happy. Even for Bill Gates there has to be a limit.

Does money buy happiness? Well, there's no doubt that an inability to pay the bills causes unhappiness. And there's no doubt, either, that having insufficient disposable income for a few of life's little pleasures causes unhappiness.

So money can certainly 'cure' some of the causes of unhappiness. But that's not the same thing at all as saying that money creates happiness. In fact, there's very little evidence for a strong positive effect of wealth on happiness. A person who earns half a million a year, isn't ten times happier than a person earning 50,000, nor even twice as happy – maybe, at a pinch, 10 per cent more happy, maybe not at all.

A survey in Britain found that 60 per cent of those in the top social classes ABC1 felt 'very pleased with things yesterday, all or most of the time' compared with 55 per cent for DEs. That's a small difference, easily explained by the fact that DEs tend to suffer the negative effects of financial hardship. In fact, in that particular survey, C2s were the happiest at 62 per cent.

The wealth required by nature is limited and is easy to procure; but the wealth required by vain ideals extends to infinity.

Epicurus (341–270 bce), Greek philosopher

A survey in America found that the very rich (incomes of over $10 million a year) were happy 77 per cent of the time, compared with 62 per cent for others chosen at random from the same area. That's a more significant difference but, again, some of the others would have faced financial problems that would have chipped away at the happiness they otherwise would have felt.

Several studies have shown that when people win large sums of money they don't become happier in the medium to longer term. Nor are people generally happier in wealthier countries compared with poorer countries. Nor does increase in national wealth result in more happiness. Americans seem to be no happier now than they were in 1946/7, and considerably less happy than they were in the late 1950s.

So, while poverty causes misery, we can dispense with wealth as a significant cause of happiness.

> **Insight**
>
> The bottom line is this: most of us are never going to be very wealthy, so the debate is academic. If you're not rich you still want to be happy. And you can be. There are other far more important things in life, and we'll be looking at these throughout this book.

Try this

1 **In Chapter 1, I advised you to keep a 'happiness diary'.** I hope that you've done this. Review it now and see where most of your happiness has been coming from. Is it from material possessions or life's inexpensive pleasures?

2 **This month, don't buy anything other than necessities and don't use any expensive products (except where you have no alternative).** Concentrate on finding happiness in things that are free or inexpensive, such as love, sex, friendship, pets, nature, swimming in the sea or a lake, walking or running, and identifying the stars.

Problem: Not wanting more is just a recipe for being a loser

Is a happy person a loser?

If it's not black, it must be white

This is a style of thinking that keeps life simple but makes no allowance for reality, which is that between black and white there are infinite shades of grey. It doesn't always cause unhappiness because there's a kind of security in it. But black-and-whiters tend to miss out on a lot. They deny themselves pleasures by saying things like, 'I'm never going to that restaurant again/speaking to him again/going to buy that brand again.'

Most of the time the black-and-white mentality leads to a good deal of misery. Either you're a success or you're a failure. Either you're attractive or you're ugly. Either you're a great raconteur or you're a bore. And since nobody is in the top drawer in every category, anyone with this outlook is going to feel despondent a lot of the time.

> Try this
> **Examine the record of the politician you hate the most.**
> You might like to buy a biography or research him or her on the Internet. Then write down the following things:
>
> ▶ *the factors in the politician's early life that influenced his or her outlook*
> ▶ *six things the politician has done that you agree with*
> ▶ *something about the politician that you like.*
>
> **Ask yourself: Do I feel happier as a result?**
> **Now try a similar exercise on yourself.** Think of something at which you've always considered yourself a complete failure, completely black (I'm hopeless at my job/conversation/ attracting the opposite sex). Then write down the following things:
>
> ▶ *the amount of training you've received*
> ▶ *the amount of effort you've made*
> ▶ *any examples of where you came somewhere between failure and success.*
>
> **Ask yourself this: Is it really all black, or a shade of grey?**

Problem: I just don't feel certain about anything any more

That's not really a problem. Once you stop dismissing people and things as 'bad' or 'evil' or 'worthless' you can begin to take pleasure in the shades of grey ('She wasn't such an awful person after all – in fact, we had quite a few laughs together.').

If it's not perfect, it's no good

You have desirable qualities if you're conscientious, meticulous and painstaking. In many jobs these are essential. But perfectionism is something different. It's striving for a level so unrealistically high, that you're either so intimidated you can't even begin, or you're reluctant ever to pronounce something 'finished'. However commendable the attitude, it has no practical use. You just end up making yourself unhappy, along with everybody else you're involved with.

You may believe, as so many do, that perfection does exist. But I'm going to prove to you that in terms of the things human beings do, it doesn't. Oh, OK, if I ask you two plus two and you answer four then, yes, that's the perfect answer. But let's look at things that are a little more complicated.

The test is this. If something is perfect it's impossible to improve it. So, let's take a look around. Let's take your TV. Is the picture quality so good it could never be improved? Obviously not. Could your car be more durable, quieter, more fuel efficient? Obviously it could. Have you ever seen a film in which every line of dialogue was convincing, every gesture accurate, every camera angle satisfying and the plot always clear? No. I won't go on. When you think about it, you'll see that perfection of that kind doesn't exist.

Obviously you have ideals of some sort. And it's important that you do. But, very often, ideals also involve a concept of perfection that's impossible to attain. Never give yourself a hard time because you fall short of those kinds of ideals. (And don't give anybody else a hard time either, because they fall short of your ideals.) Rather, congratulate yourself when you move closer to your ideals. Or, better still, set yourself ideals that are realistic.

Some gurus say that perfection does exist. There are even those mystics who say that everything is perfect. We just don't see it because of our pre-existing ideas of how things should be.

Insight

Have you ever been to a dog show? And been mystified as to why one dog is proclaimed almost perfect while another lovely dog is eliminated? Think about it. It's only to do with artificial rules invented by people. Change the rules and the losing dog becomes the winner. Becomes 'perfect'.

Try this

1 **Whatever you have to do today, set out to do it to a good and competent standard, but not to perfection.** At the end of the day, work out how much you got through compared with a perfectionist day.

2 **Try coming at the situation from a completely different tack.** Try to see that things you've been dismissing as imperfect are, in fact, perfect in their way. For example, take a look at yourself in the mirror. Too short at 5′ 2″? Who says? In fact, you're a perfect example of a person of 5′ 2″. Too many freckles? Who says? In fact, you're a perfect example of freckles. Bald? You're a perfect example of baldness. So now go out in the garden and learn to see that everything there is a perfect and unique example of itself – each flower different, each flower perfect.

Problem: If I don't deliver perfection I'm worried I'll get the sack

If you think you've been delivering perfection up till now then I've got news for you – you're mistaken! But, of course, you didn't really think that, did you? No human being ever delivers perfection. But by striving for perfection and thinking you must achieve perfection you're creating a barrier. In my profession we call it 'writer's block'. It's when you're so anxious to create a masterpiece that you can't actually function at all. Believe me, the people who pay you are going to be far happier if you produce three pieces of competent work, rather than one piece of 'perfect' work.

Why is this *always* happening to me?

Most of us focus far too much on the negative and, what's more, exaggerate the significance of anything that goes wrong. The whole thing is summed up in that well-known phrase: Why is this *always* happening to me?

We get angry (see Chapter 4) and allow our emotions to build and cloud our judgement.

You know the kind of thing. You get a bird-dropping on your clothes and you say it. You get a puncture and you say it. You get a parking ticket and you say it. And yet it's never true. You get a parking ticket once a year, a bird-dropping on your clothes once in five years and a puncture once a decade.

Insight

What makes you notice the bad things is not that they always happen, but that they happen *so seldom*. In fact, if they always happened you wouldn't bother to mention the subject.

Problem: I couldn't think of anything to write about myself

If you really can't think of anything then you're being too hard on yourself. In fact, if your sheet of paper is blank or only has a couple of points written on it then we don't have to look very far for one of the sources of your unhappiness. You don't like yourself enough. You don't love yourself enough. Well, you should. For a start, you're certainly modest. So put that down. You're obviously sensitive. So put that down. You're also introspective. Add that to the list. That's three useful qualities already.

Many unhappy people simply demand too much of themselves and those around them, too. We're all human beings – animals, in fact – with enormous limitations. You're going to have to learn to accept that about yourself

(Contd)

and your fellow man and woman. Just do your best.
Nobody can ask more. Now get back to the list and don't
stop until you've got at least 20 things written down.

When you've finished writing about yourself, make a list of all the
good points about your partner. Again, here are some suggestions
to get you going:

- ▶ *He/she seldom gets angry.*
- ▶ *He/she never spends money without discussing it with me first.*
- ▶ *He/she is always very considerate towards my parents.*
- ▶ *He/she looks after me when I'm ill.*
- ▶ *He/she likes many of the same things I do.*
- ▶ *He/she makes me laugh.*
- ▶ *He/she cooks beautiful meals for me.*

And then do the same for your children, your parents and anyone
else you're close to.

Problem: I couldn't think of anything to write about people close to me

If you really can't think of anything then it's not just a
question of being too hard on the people around you.
There's obviously some kind of deep resentment at work

(Contd)

because everybody has good qualities, even if they have a few bad ones, too. And you're going to have to discharge that resentment. We'll be taking a deeper look at your relationships in Chapter 9.

Next, you're going to make a list of all the good things in your life. For example:

- *I'm in good health.*
- *I have somewhere nice to live.*
- *I never have to go hungry.*
- *I have many friends.*

Now make your list. Begin with your body. If it works pretty much as it should, then that's already something to be very happy about. Can you see? Can you hear? Can you touch things? Can you taste things? Can you smell them? Can you remember things? Can you run? Can you swim? Can you make love? This is going to be a pretty long list.

Problem: My list is very short

Nobody's list should – could – be short. If yours is then you've got to learn to appreciate things more than you do. You're taking far too much for granted. You've got to learn to stop comparing with the ultimate – the richest person, the biggest house, the strongest athlete, the most beautiful face – and try to get a bit more perspective. Don't forget that there are also people who have almost nothing to eat, who don't have any kind of house and who combat severe disabilities.

When you've finished your lists, copy them out very clearly onto some card or, if you have a computer, print them. Also make the 'highlights' into a portable version you can keep in your wallet or

handbag. Make sure you always have copies close to hand.
Here's what you do.

- ▶ *When you get up in the morning, read the lists.*
- ▶ *When you're having lunch, read the lists.*
- ▶ *Just before you go to sleep, read the lists.*
- ▶ *Any time you're feeling unhappy or cross with your partner or people close to you, read the lists.*

Insight

It probably sounds a rather silly idea to make lists of positive things, but it's been proven to work in many experiments. In fact, it's an extremely powerful technique for achieving happiness. So do try it. And not just for a day. It's going to take your brain some time to rewire itself with this new and more positive way of looking at the world. Try it for at least a month.

I'm not going to like this

Your partner is late. You look at your watch and begin to get angry. A little while later your anger starts to become overlaid by concern. 'He's had an accident.' 'She's been abducted.' You're worried and very unhappy.

After an hour your partner arrives. What happened? It turns out to have been nothing more than a simple misunderstanding over the time. One of you thought you'd agreed on 8 o'clock, the other 9 o'clock.

These kinds of situations happen. The people whispering in the corner, who – you convince yourself – are saying bad things about you. The boss who doesn't greet you in the usual, cheerful way because – you convince yourself – he's about to reprimand you. The medical test, which – you convince yourself – is bound to have found a life-threatening condition.

In the same vein, we all also like to have a go at predicting the future, and enjoy saying 'I told you so' when our forecasts turn out to be right. And the predictions are usually negative. But we tend to forget the occasions when we were wrong. If you're someone who always has a negative view of things you may be surprised how many times that happens. Let's find out.

Try this

Carry a notebook with you for the next week. Every time a negative prediction comes into your mind, write it down. Things like:

▶ *I'm never going to be able to do this.*
▶ *He's going to cause trouble for me.*
▶ *She isn't going to like me.*
▶ *They look very suspicious.*
▶ *There's no way out of this.*
▶ *It can only mean something terrible has happened.*

When the outcome of the situation is known, write it in your notebook. At the end of the week, tot up how many times your negative predictions turned out to be right and how many wrong. You'll almost certainly find the latter outweigh the former by a considerable margin. That's an awful lot of anxiety over nothing. Now try writing down positive predictions and see how many times they come true. Yes, more often than you think!

Problem: If I don't anticipate the worst I can't defend myself against it

If you've done the exercise above you'll know that your negative outlook just isn't in accordance with reality. You're wasting a lot of energy and making yourself unhappy quite needlessly. Look at it this way. What have you got to lose

(Contd)

by adopting a positive stance? 'The people in the corner are discussing their sex lives.' 'The boss is preoccupied.' 'The results of my medical test will be fine.' Of course, there are occasions when it would be prudent to take some action, but you can still do that without having to visualize worst-case scenarios. Believe the best until you have reason to know otherwise.

I feel it, so it must be true

The ugly duckling that becomes a swan is a story that goes back as long as stories have been told. The duckling feels ugly (usually because of things others have said) and comes to believe it must be true. And so it can be with many other emotions. You feel like a failure and conclude that you are a failure. You feel that nobody likes you and conclude that you're unlovable. You feel you can't cope and conclude you're a bad mother. But your feelings can be wrong. For sure, you're far more of a swan than you realize.

> ### Try this
> **Next time you feel the kinds of emotions that undermine your self-esteem, write them down.** Then try to analyse the situation objectively. If you can't, enlist the help of a friend. Write down six reasons why your emotion wasn't justified.

Problem: I'm a very intuitive person and I don't think I should ignore my intuitions

Intuitions should never be ignored. But this is something different. We're concerned here with your emotions about yourself that simply aren't justified.

I'm a label; you're a label

As with the black and white approach, labels can make life simpler. I'm a loser. He's an idiot. She's stupid. They're unbeatable. Once the label has been decided, there's no need to look any more deeply or keep the situation under review. And that's exactly why labelling is a disaster. It's far too simplistic, takes no account of change and, worst of all, is self-fulfilling.

For example, when you go to play the tennis partners who are 'unbeatable' you'll have given up before even hitting the first ball. When you decide you're a 'loser' you won't even try any more. And when you treat other people as 'idiots' you don't give them the opportunity to tackle problems and grow.

> *The only person who acts sensibly is my tailor. He takes my measure anew every time he sees me. Everyone else goes by their old measurements.*
>
> George Bernard Shaw (1836–1950), Irish dramatist

> ## Try this
> 1 **Write down the names of all the people to whom you've attributed labels.** Include yourself, if you've given yourself a label. Next to the names write the label. Now, in each case, find six reasons why the label is inappropriate.
> 2 **Choose a subject at which you've labelled yourself a failure and given up trying** (I can't dance/play tennis/do maths, or whatever). Then take lessons from a properly qualified teacher. You may not be the best, but you'll discover that you're certainly not a 'failure' either.

I should do this; you should do that

We all have a little voice within telling us what we should do. (And quite often it's reinforced by someone else's voice, too.)

I should cut the grass, even though it's only an inch long. I should clean the house, even though I did it last week. I should go to Bill and Sheila's party, even though we have nothing in common. And when you don't do what you should, you feel guilt. Guilt is a very unpleasant emotion to have to deal with, and I'll have more to say about it in the next chapter.

Maybe you also direct 'should statements' at others. You should smarten yourself up a bit. You should go to the funeral. You should get a better job. If the people you're directing the statements at don't take any notice, you end up feeling frustrated and resentful.

> ### Try this
> **For the next week, banish all 'shoulds' and see what happens.** Each time you're faced with a 'should situation', apply a different mindset to it: 'Taking all things into account, will I be happier if I do this or if I don't?'
> **As regards other people, ask yourself this: 'What right have I got to tell someone else what to do?'**

Problem: Sometimes there just are things you've got to do, whether you like it or not

Yes. But far fewer than you think. We're concerned with happiness, not 'should'.

If it's wrong, it must be my fault

Accepting responsibility for things that aren't your responsibility is a common error, particularly among women. Women are the nurturing sex, so it's understandable that they react this way more often than men do.

Let's say that your elderly father insists on driving. He hasn't had an accident yet, but you're convinced it's only a matter of time – and not very much time. You feel it's your responsibility to tell him to sell the car. You lay awake at night worrying about how to persuade him – and how he'll manage without it. You're unhappy.

But let's look at the facts. Your father is an adult, with more experience than you have, and makes his own decisions. He hasn't had an accident, which probably means he's acknowledged his limitations and drives accordingly. The police haven't interfered. His doctor hasn't interfered. So why should you?

> ## Try this
> **Make a checklist of 25 things involving other people that you consider yourself to be responsible for (for example, ironing his shirts, checking that your partner is 'correctly' dressed, making sure the kids do their homework).** Then go through the list asking yourself:
>
> ▶ *Am I really responsible for this?*
> ▶ *Why can't the other person do this for him/herself?*
> ▶ *In what way am I so superior that only I can do this?*
> ▶ *In what way is the other person so inferior as to be incapable of doing this?*

Problem: When I love someone it's only right that I should intervene

You're going to have to accept that there are things beyond your control and that other people have free will and ideas of their own. Quite possibly, you like the feeling that other people can't do without you and that you're indispensable.

(Contd)

That's not a terrible thing. The problem comes when you start to worry and make yourself unhappy over something that really isn't your responsibility.

Insight

We all have an inner voice, almost like an independent person living inside us. When that inner voice is critical, it tends to make us unhappy and demoralized. Perhaps it says, 'You idiot, you're always doing stupid things like that.' You know the kind of thing. Try talking back to the voice just as if it were another person. It's not a sign of madness. Ask it, 'Why are you saying things like that when they aren't justified?' Question it. 'What are you hoping to achieve by being so critical?' Debate with it. 'Wouldn't it be more helpful to congratulate me when I do well?' Aim to convert your inner voice, over time, into one that's more positive, optimistic and cheerful.

Applying the lessons to your past

We've started to work on your present and future. But what about your past? Does your past bother you? Does it make you unhappy? Then why not change it? Let's apply some of the lessons we've just learned.

But surely, you say, we can't change our past lives? Surely we can't change the facts of history? Well, no, we can't change the facts, but are you sure they are the facts? We only remember a tiny fraction of past events and, to some extent, we choose our memories to fit with the world view we've selected for ourselves. Some people choose to remember the best and some choose to remember the worst.

Are you, for example, one of the many people who has been through a separation or divorce? What, then, are your memories of your ex-partner? Can you remember that you once loved him or her? Or can you only recall the rows and the flying saucepans? Do you only *want* to remember the rows and the flying saucepans? That's most likely the case. But there was a time when you were in love. There was a time when you were happy together. Why not remember those times?

It doesn't mean pretending the bad things never happened. You may, indeed, have to face up to those bad things and deal with them. But it may be that you have feelings of bitterness and resentment that are spoiling your present life, and yet which aren't justified. There is a different way of looking back at things. Consider these statements, for example:

- ▶ *I should never have married, but then, inevitably we make mistakes when we're young.*
- ▶ *We had some good years together.*
- ▶ *We had some difficult times but I learned from them.*
- ▶ *It's fortunate we split up because I'm now able to fulfil myself in a more suitable relationship.*
- ▶ *I've made my new relationship much stronger than it ever would have been, if I didn't have those past experiences to draw on.*

These are all positive ways of looking at the past. You'll be much happier if you adopt the same mindset.

Insight

Your past can be a rich source of pleasure if you allow it to be. Don't cut yourself off from it simply because a few things turned out badly. Yes, looking back can make you feel bitter. But it can also make you extremely happy. It's your *choice*.

Peter's story

CASE STUDY

For a long time I've felt rather bitter about my schooldays. I didn't like the rules. I thought they were very unjust, and looking back made me angry. Then I realized that, intended or not, my school days made me into a person who has fought against injustice ever since. I realized I should be grateful. And now I am.

Insight

If you're having a problem with a particular bad memory, you may be able to desensitize yourself through the power of music. Here's how. Recall the scene and, at the same time, 'play' some music in your mind that is completely incongruous. In most cases you'll want it to be something humorous –

perhaps the theme from your favourite comedy programme. In other words, it's as if you're watching a film with the wrong soundtrack. Do this several times. Check your response by recalling the scene again, but this time without the music. Hopefully you'll find you're a lot less upset by the memory than you had been.

In this chapter we've looked at negative thought patterns. Try to banish them. Practise the exercises regularly. In the next chapter we'll learn to do the same with negative emotions.

10 THINGS TO REMEMBER

1 *You are what you think. So, think exclusively happy thoughts – about the past as well as the present and the future – and you'll become a profoundly happy person.*

2 *If you must compare, only compare with people worse off than you; in fact, wealth has little to do with happiness and, anyway, greed can never be satisfied.*

3 *Real life is shades of grey, not black and white.*

4 *It's pointless aiming for perfection because it's impossible to achieve.*

5 *Your negative thoughts are inevitably exaggerated.*

6 *Predictions of disaster seldom come true.*

7 *Don't always believe your emotions.*

8 *Don't stick labels on people or yourself – they're never correct.*

9 *You don't have to do what you should, so much as what makes you happy.*

10 *Don't take responsibility for things that aren't your responsibility.*

HOW HAPPY ARE YOU NOW?

Now that you've read in detail about the ten negative ways of thinking, what do you feel about them?

a *I agree that some are negative but I still see others as positive.*
b *I agree they're all negative but, in practice, I just can't react as I should.*
c *I've now stopped thinking in any of those negative ways.*

I certainly wouldn't expect anybody to answer '(c)' at this stage, but if you did, or if you agreed that most of the ten ways of thinking were negative, then you're ready to move on to Chapter 4.

If, however, you think most of the ten ways of thinking are actually positive, then you're not yet completely focused on happiness. Yes, comparing with others often acts as a spur to strive harder; yes, greed is often an ingredient in amassing enormous wealth; yes, perfectionism may lead to a great work of art – eventually. But we're concerned with happiness, not with getting rich or having a painting in a famous art gallery. Being consistently happy requires a different mindset.

Spend a little time reflecting on what you really want in life. Are you going to sacrifice happiness to achieve other goals? Or are you going to make happiness your goal?

Keep smiling

Welcome to the psychotherapy hotline:

If you are obsessive-compulsive, please press 1 repeatedly.

If you are co-dependent, please ask someone to press 2.

If you have multiple personalities, please press 3, 4, 5 and 6.

If you are schizophrenic, listen carefully and a little voice will tell you which number to press.

If you are depressed it really doesn't matter what number you select because no one will answer anyway.

4

Goodbye to negative emotions

In this chapter you will learn:
- *how negative emotions can harm you*
- *the antidotes to negative emotions*
- *how laughter can beat stress.*

> *I like living. I have sometimes been wildly, despairingly, acutely miserable, racked with sorrow, but through it all I still know quite certainly that just to be alive is a grand thing.*
>
> Agatha Christie (1890–1976), English crime writer

In the previous chapter I looked at unhappy, negative ways of thinking and how to change them. In this chapter I'm going to look at unhappy, negative emotions and how you can overcome them. If you don't, the person they'll harm is you.

I've selected ten emotions that can damage your life. There are others, but I'm focusing on these because in our society, to a greater or lesser extent, they're often considered to be prudent, appropriate and even beneficial. You've probably lived with them all your life, and never questioned them – until now.

Potentially damaging emotions

Some harmful emotions	anger, blame, cynicism, hate, revenge, jealousy, resentment, suspicion, indifference, guilt
The antidotes	empathy, understanding, sympathy, patience, tolerance, kindness, forgiveness

Insight

You're probably going to find some of the ideas strange at first. They're far from the normal Western way of looking at things. And they can seem to demand almost superhuman qualities. But try this new way and you may be surprised to find it easier than you imagined. And the rewards, in terms of happiness, are enormous.

Feeling good about other people

Anger builds more anger. And more anger builds hate. There's quite a lot of scientific data to prove it, but it's not really necessary to refer to that to know that it's true. We all know how we can 'goad' ourselves on. And we also know how other people respond. In Oriental thought, as well as physics, every force creates an equal and opposite force.

It's one of the most important lessons you can learn when dealing with yourself and with other people. Anger is the way to escalate a situation, both internally and externally. The idea that you can get rid of your anger by letting it out is a popular one, but misguided. Shouting at somebody, or shouting at an empty chair which represents somebody, or punching pillows, is the exact opposite of what's needed. The best way to counter anger is to understand the other person's position. In other words, let the other person explain why they said or did what they did and, if you still feel angry, explain in turn how you feel and why. This is completely different from venting your anger, as if it's steam escaping from a pressure cooker. What you actually need to do is turn off the heat.

If you are going to let your anger out then let it out as laughter (see later in this chapter). There's another very good reason to eliminate negative emotions. Quite simply, negative emotions make you ill.

Insight

From what you now know about the workings of your brain you can see the danger. When you allow your anger to build up you're actually strengthening the 'anger synapses' in your brain. You're moulding your brain for anger. Far from getting rid of the anger, you're unintentionally redesigning the capacity of your brain to create more anger. It's a disaster, because when you're angry you can't be happy.

How negative emotions are dangerous for your health

Negative emotions are assassins. And the person they're stalking is you.

A link between emotion and illness has long been postulated, but it was only in the 1970s that a psychologist called Robert Ader uncovered one of the mechanisms. He gave rats saccharin-flavoured water along with a chemical that suppressed T-cells. Later he gave just the saccharin-flavoured water but the rats' T-cell count still went down. The significance of the experiment was that it proved a connection between the brain (which 'tasted' the water) and the immune system.

Soon afterwards, a colleague at the School of Medicine and Dentistry, University of Rochester, by the name of David Felten, pinpointed synapse-like contacts where the autonomic nervous system (responsible for 'running' the body) spoke to the immune cells using neurotransmitters.

There's at least one other mechanism connecting emotions and physical health. During stress, the body releases a cocktail of hormones including adrenaline (epinephrine), noradrenaline (norepinephrine), cortisol and prolactin. Generally speaking, these 'stress hormones' have the effect of suppressing the immune system. Why evolution should have arranged things that way can only be conjectured. Possibly it's a method of conserving energy during an emergency.

The problem is that if stress is prolonged or constant (if, for example, you nurture your negative emotions) then your immune system will be permanently compromised.

What's more, stress hormones lead to higher levels of glucose, cholesterol and fat in the blood to provide the energy for physical action. But if physical action doesn't follow (and, in our society, it usually doesn't), plaque is deposited on the walls of the blood vessels. To that long-term risk can be added the short-term risk of heart attack, when noradrenaline levels are sharply elevated.

A list of the disorders related to negative emotions includes: allergies, asthma, cancers, colds and flu, depression, diabetes, headaches, heart disease, hypertension, indigestion, muscle pain and cramps, sexual problems, strokes and ulcers.

The conclusion is simple: be happy, stay healthy.

Insight

Look upon your peace of mind and happiness as a great treasure that has to be protected at all costs. It's not something with which you can take risks. Think of it like one of your children. Or the greatest love of your life. When anything threatens it, take evasive action immediately.

Learning to empathize

The way to protect your peace of mind and happiness is with empathy. Don't make the mistake of thinking that empathy is primarily for the benefit of another person: empathy is for your benefit. Let's take a simple everyday example.

Your partner dents the car. You become angry. Why? Did your partner do it intentionally? Of course not. Have you ever dented a car? Possibly. Will you dent a car some time in the future? Probably. Will your anger make the dent disappear? Absolutely not. So what purpose is served by your anger? What benefit does it bring you or anybody else? The truth is that it does you harm.

Ask yourself these questions:

▶ *How would I have felt if I'd dented the car?*
▶ *How must my partner have felt?*
▶ *How would I like to be treated if I dented the car?*

In other words, you need to empathize, that's to say, imaginatively enter into another person's situation.

Insight
Millions of people have died because others lacked empathy. Anger built more anger, which built hate. And hate led to killing on a massive scale. You only have to look at conflicts all over the world, past and present, to understand this.

Keep smiling
Confucius say, when you are angry at a neighbour walk a mile in his shoes.

Then you'll be a mile away... and you'll have his shoes.

Try this

For the next week, do your best to empathize with everyone you're in contact with, especially anyone with whom you're in conflict. When someone is angry with you, do your best not to get angry back. Just as you can 'send' your mind to a part of your own body to see how it feels, 'send' your mind into the other person to see how they feel (there's more on this in Chapter 6).

Before you ask any questions out loud, try to imagine why the person is behaving as they are. Don't label them as, say, troublemakers or neurotics, and don't try to reduce the situation to an issue of black-and-white, but look for the grey (see Chapter 3 if you've forgotten about these negative thought patterns). Start from the position that the other person is a perfectly reasonable human being (normally a correct assumption) and must have a valid reason for their behaviour.

Now, in a calm tone of voice, ask questions. How do you see the situation? What would you like to do about it? What is it that's making you angry? Why are you so upset about this?

When the other person replies, don't focus on the things you disagree with. Instead, do your best to find something to agree with.

When you do this, you'll defuse the other person's anger as well as your own. Then, with both of you in a more positive frame of mind, you can start to sort out the areas of disagreement. And, it's hoped, reach a happy conclusion.

Let's say, for example, you've been asked to do something in connection with work. You haven't done it for sound professional reasons. But, for the moment, you haven't got much chance to go into that because the other person is really angry and aggressive (too much testosterone, as we'll see in the next chapter). Read these responses:

Other person: 'You're utterly incompetent!'

You: 'I can understand why you feel that way.'

Other person: 'Can't you ever do anything right?'

You: 'I agree that I haven't done what you asked.'

It isn't easy to respond like this but, if you do, the other person is almost certainly going to calm down a bit. Having diffused the situation you can then go on to explain:

You: 'I have to do what's correct and on this occasion...'

The other person is behaving badly, but it isn't going to help the situation if you do the same. You know the problems you've encountered, but the other person doesn't... yet!

Of course, you could have responded in kind:

You (shouting): 'You're the one who's incompetent! Your instructions were stupid.'

But that's hardly likely to lead to happiness for anyone.

Now let's turn it around. This time it's you who's asked for something to be done and it's the other person who, apparently, has failed to do it. But your approach is going to be very different:

You: 'I note that you haven't yet done that job I asked you to do. Is there some problem that we need to discuss?'

Other person: 'I'm very glad you've asked me that because, actually, there is.'

Now you have the opportunity to resolve the situation together and maybe you can learn something as a result. You'll find that happiness is far more likely to come from

(Contd)

sympathizing with the person who has 'failed' than from being critical:

▶ The other person will be a friend rather than an enemy.
▶ The other person will be more likely to treat you reasonably when you 'fail'.
▶ You'll have no reason to feel negative emotions, which are destructive.

Insight

Some people secretly welcome other people's failures because they can then take pleasure in being superior. But that isn't the way to happiness. Instead, take pleasure in being helpful.

Problem: Everyone is going to think I'm weak

Not at all. On the contrary, they're going to admire your insight, wisdom and, above all, your imperturbability. Consider this situation. Let's say you go to a pub for a quiet drink. In the bar there's a man who's drunk and aggressive. He insults you, hoping for a fight. What do you do? What's strong and what's weak? Here's a clue. If you fight him, you've let him dictate how your evening will proceed.

Blame, resentment and revenge

Ideally you need to resolve a situation when it occurs without carrying any emotional poisons with you into the future. But so often it isn't like that. Let's take a common relationship problem. One partner suggests sex and the other then announces a headache. As a result, the first partner sulks.

This is the thinking: 'This is *always* happening. My partner never wants to have sex with me, doesn't like sex and obviously has a problem. It's clear my partner doesn't really love me at all. I'm looking for the world's greatest love affair and this clearly isn't it. This relationship is a waste of time.'

(You'll recognize the negative styles of thinking from Chapter 3, including black-and-white, exaggeration, jumping to negative conclusions, perfectionism and labelling.)

The result is resentment and a desire for revenge, with thoughts like:

▶ *I can't be treated like that.*
▶ *I'll teach my partner a lesson.*
▶ *I'll make my partner suffer.*
▶ *I'll pay my partner back several times over.*

These are particularly destructive emotions, especially in a relationship. If you think in these kinds of terms you cause immense unhappiness not only for your partner, but also for yourself. While you have those kinds of thoughts you just can't be happy.

It's easy to see why. You:

▶ *cut yourself off from your partner's company*
▶ *stop enjoying things together*
▶ *deny yourself physical contact*
▶ *prolong negative emotions for hours or even days*
▶ *make yourself physically ill.*

In short, to use an old cliché, you 'cut off your nose to spite your face'.

The right course is to accept that your partner does have a headache. You should ask if there's anything you can do (a painkiller, a cup of tea, taking over your partner's chores). All the while, you should be thinking like this: 'My partner and I have been together for years and we've had some incredible sex. I love my partner and I know my partner loves me and wouldn't deliberately do anything to upset me. We can't expect to be perfectly synchronized for sex. That's asking the impossible.'

As a result of which, you remain happy and probably enjoy sex a few hours later.

Keep smiling

I have never hated a man enough to give him back his diamonds.

Zsa Zsa Gabor (1917–), Hungarian–American actress

Try this

Would you accept that you're especially sensitive about certain issues? That you have the odd weakness or two? That you're inhibited in certain areas? Then next time you have a disagreement with someone, remember you both have vulnerabilities and weaknesses.

So, rather than focusing on theirs, begin with your own. Don't list their failings in your mind – list your own failings. Not, that is, in a self-critical way. Just remind yourself, for the purpose of balance, that you also sometimes make mistakes and that that's perfectly normal. Your desire for revenge will go.

Because someone doesn't behave as you want doesn't mean they're deliberately out to oppose you. Some issue in their lives may be inhibiting them. Do your best to help other people tackle the issues in their lives.

To err is human, to forgive divine

A very wise saying because forgiving is extremely good for your health and happiness. And not forgiving can cause anxiety, depression, heart problems, chronic pain and premature death. Put like that, there's really no argument.

▶ *Forgive – stop turning the situation over in your mind and let it go.*
▶ *When it's you who's in the wrong, apologize without making excuses.*

Insight

A useful technique for letting go is dissociating. When we're really annoyed or upset about something then, in our minds, we see it 'close up'. We make it as vivid as possible and, consequently, make our emotions equally strong. In order to let go you need to do the opposite. You need to dissociate as far as possible by pulling back the 'camera' of your mind's eye, just as a camera pulls back in a film. As a result, your negative emotions will be much weaker and more easily dealt with. It's a particularly useful technique for handling unhappy situations about which, in practical terms, you can do absolutely nothing.

Feeling good about yourself

If you feel guilty, give yourself a pat on the back. Congratulations. You're a member of the human race and a creditable one at that. Of course you feel guilt. A person who doesn't is known as a psychopath. But there's no point in hating yourself either. Everybody makes mistakes. You can't be blamed for that.

If your guilt becomes a source of discouragement and ultimately depression, then you can't function to the benefit of other people. That would be adding another mistake on top of the earlier ones.

One of life's great paradoxes is that it's the most thoughtful people who tend to be the least satisfied with themselves.

Keep smiling

A woman goes to see a psychotherapist.

'Every time I date someone I end up sleeping with him and then in the morning I feel guilty and depressed.'

'I see,' says the psychotherapist. 'And you want me to strengthen your resolve.'

'No, no! I want you to fix it so I don't feel guilty any more.'

If you're hard on yourself it means you recognize the need to grow. Growing is, itself, a generator of happiness. Be happy that you still have a journey to make – a hugely enjoyable journey.

As the old saying goes, nobody is perfect. Buddhists believe that's why you have to keep returning to Earth so you can progress further. The Buddhists say nobody can achieve perfection in one lifetime and, whether you believe in reincarnation or not, that much is certainly true.

Remember that success is a very poor teacher. Success never requires that you examine yourself. Failure, on the other hand, is a very good teacher. Never be afraid of failure – just make sure you learn from it.

Insight

Nobody has really failed until they give up. So don't give up. You may fail to climb a mountain today but you could be on the summit next month or next year. As long as you keep learning and keep trying there's always a chance.

It is not how much we have, but how much we enjoy, that makes happiness.

Charles Spurgeon (1834–92), English preacher

Try this

The idea of this exercise is to understand how your failures have actually been positive experiences. Begin by heading up a sheet of paper with 'Failures' on the left-hand side and 'Benefits' on the right-hand side. Now write down everything you consider to have been a failure. When you've finished, go back to the beginning, and against each failure list all the lessons you've learned from it.

The stress buster

Back in Chapter 1 I advised you to practise smiling even when you don't have a reason to smile. I hope you've been doing this, because now I'm going to ask you to do something even harder. I want you to laugh without having any particular reason to laugh.

Why? Because laughter is a great stress buster. It can de-stress you. It can de-stress other people. It can de-stress the whole situation. And the easier you can turn it on the better. It doesn't even have to be 'authentic' laughter. As we all know, a placebo – pretend medicine – can prove highly effective. And pretend laughter is the same. What's more, it can do something a placebo can't. It can turn itself into the real thing. Start laughing and, quite soon, you – and everyone else – may find it's the genuine article.

*We don't laugh because we're not happy, we are happy
because we laugh.*

William James (1842–1910),
American psychologist

*Laughter doesn't need a reason to be – in fact, laughter is
unreasonable, illogical and irrational. Laughter exists for its
own sake.*

Annette Goodheart, PhD, laughter specialist

Insight

I'd like you to laugh right now. Don't worry if there are
other people around. They'll simply assume you're reading a
very funny book. In fact, if you're in a public place, maybe a
train, hold the book up so everyone can see it and really give
your best belly laugh. Did you do it? Then, thanks for the
advertisement.

40 laughs a day

When we're young, laughter comes fairly easily. It starts as early
as three weeks, according to some scientists, and certainly by four
months. (Unfortunately, as far as is known, no baby ever learned to
laugh before it learned to cry.)

Small children laugh around 40 times a day, but as we get older
we laugh less. One researcher has concluded that adults in the
West laugh an average of just 17 times a day. That's not actually
very much. Little more than once an hour, in fact. I'm aiming to
get you laughing at least those 40 times a day you enjoyed as
a child.

It's not just for you. It's for everyone you come in contact
with as well. Because what goes around, comes around.
The happier you can make other people, the happier they can
make you.

GET INTO TRAINING

If you're going to smile, laugh and be happy more than ever before, you've got to get into training. If you were strengthening your biceps, you'd pick up weights even though you didn't actually want them, in other words, for no reason. It's the same with smiling and laughter. You've got to learn to smile for no reason. You've got to learn to laugh for no reason.

Then, in the same way that you can become capable of lifting heavier and heavier weights, so you can become capable of smiling and laughing in 'heavier and heavier' situations.

I learned this lesson years ago from a woman who taught children with a wide range of disabilities. She was always smiling, always laughing in the midst of difficulties and, at first, it annoyed me. How could everything seem so funny to her? How could she be so insensitive to all the problems of her pupils, let alone the rest of the world? It seemed to be a kind of madness.

One day, perhaps reading my mind, she explained it to me. Many of her pupils with quite severe disabilities were nevertheless happy. How could she not be happy with all the advantages she had? And then I saw very clearly my own disability. She had pupils who, for example, couldn't walk without callipers. In my case, I couldn't be happy, couldn't laugh, unless I, too, was provided with artificial assistance.

She wasn't mad at all. She was one of the few sane people. It's the rest of us who are mad. If we need assistance to laugh and be happy then we, too, are disabled. So practise your unassisted laughing and cure your disability.

Laughter really is the best medicine

You probably don't need convincing that laughter is good for you. But I'm going to tell you anyway: laugh and you're less likely to get ill; if you are ill, you'll get better more quickly.

That's why in hospitals, clinics and social centres in more than 50 countries there are now more than 5,000 laughter clubs. Some were inspired by Dr Madan Kataria who created World Laughter Day in 1998. According to Dr Kataria, our great-grandparents used to laugh four times more than we do. That's hard to prove, but the benefits of laughing are not, as we'll be seeing in a moment. To capture those benefits Dr Kataria invented Laughter Yoga – a combination of laughter with yoga breathing – and recommends 20 minutes a day.

But probably the most influential name in 'laughter therapy' today is that of Norman Cousins.

NORMAN COUSINS

Norman Cousins was diagnosed with an extremely painful type of arthritis known as Ankylosing Spondylitis and was told he had only a one in 500 chance of recovery. Till that moment he'd been content to let the doctors get on with it. That all changed when he heard the prognosis, as he recalled in his famous book *Anatomy of an Illness*. 'I felt a compulsion to get into the act,' he wrote. 'It seemed clear to me that if I was to be that one in 500 I had better be something more than a passive observer.'

His active role was to prescribe himself large doses of vitamin C and regular injections of Marx Brothers' films. 'I made the joyous discovery,' he wrote, 'that ten minutes of genuine belly laughter had an anaesthetic effect and would give me at least two hours of pain-free sleep.'

Norman Cousins may sound like a crackpot but he certainly wasn't. When he died in 1990 he had a distinguished career behind him as a long-time editor of the New York-based *Saturday Review*, had been a leading activist for nuclear disarmament and world peace, and had spent his retirement as a faculty member of the University of California at the Los Angeles School of Medicine studying the relationship between attitude and health. His experience certainly raised the profile of 'laughter therapy', although it still isn't the universal treatment it should be.

Insight

Some doubt has now been cast on the accuracy of the original diagnosis. But that isn't the most important point. The truly important point is that Norman Cousins was in severe pain and that laughter reduced or even halted it, at least for a while.

WHAT HAPPENS WHEN YOU LAUGH?

Let's first of all trace what happens in the brain when you hear a good joke.

▶ *An electrical wave moves through the cerebral cortex (the largest part of the brain) within less than half a second of seeing or hearing something potentially funny.*

- *The left side of the cortex analyses the joke or situation.*
- *Activity increases in the frontal lobe.*
- *The occipital lobe processes any visual signals.*
- *The right hemisphere of the cortex is where you 'get' the joke.*
- *The most 'primitive' part of the brain – the limbic system (especially amygdala and hippocampus) – is involved in the emotional response.*
- *The hypothalamus is involved in the production of loud, uncontrollable laughter.*

So your brain is getting a good workout, for a start.

In turn, the laughter:

- *increases the disease-fighting protein Gamma-interferon*
- *increases T-cells and B-cells, which make disease-fighting antibodies*
- *increases immunoglobulin A, the body's first line of defence against infections of the upper respiratory tract*
- *increases immunoglobulins M and G*
- *increases Complement 3, which helps antibodies pierce defective or infected cells in order to destroy them*
- *benefits anyone suffering from diabetes because it lowers blood sugar*
- *benefits the heart*
- *lowers blood pressure (after an initial increase)*
- *lowers stress hormones, including cortisol*
- *strengthens abdominal muscles*
- *relaxes the body*
- *reduces pain, possibly by the production of endorphins, but certainly through relaxation and distraction*
- *flushes water vapour from the lungs*
- *speeds recovery from surgery, especially for children.*

One extra reason to laugh:

- *It stops everyone thinking you're dull.*

And one reason not to:

▶ *Your underwear may get damp.*

A clown is like an aspirin, only he works twice as fast.

Groucho Marx (1890–1977), American comedian

Tip

If you're in pain you may be able to use laughter in a very specific way. Do something to increase the pain. Yes, increase it. If it's an arthritic joint, for example, move it. If it's an injury, press it. Then laugh. Keep on doing it. Pain. Laugh. Pain. Laugh. Pain. Laugh. After a while, you won't feel the pain so much.

Warning – laughing can sometimes be a bad thing
There are just a few medical conditions that could be made worse by too much laughing. If you're asthmatic, laughing just might trigger an attack. It can also be bad for anyone with a serious heart condition, a hernia, severe piles, certain eye problems, and anyone who has just undergone abdominal surgery.

Don't just sit there, tell a joke

We've talked about laughing for no particular reason. Now let's talk about you creating genuinely funny situations. If you have a like-minded family and friends they'll follow your lead and, with luck, none of you will ever stop laughing.

▶ *Buy some books of jokes, practise the ones you like, then try them out on your friends.*
▶ *Learn to be playful.*

Tip

If you've ever wondered how other people come up with witty ripostes so quickly, the answer is that they don't. They've been learning them in secret ready for use when the right circumstances present themselves. You can do the same. Once you've learned some basic jokes and one-liners from joke books, practise adapting them to different situations. When I was a skinny young man, a friend told me: 'You're so thin you must have to run around in the shower to get wet.' I was deeply impressed ... until I saw the repeat of the TV programme from which he'd stolen the gag.

Don't say you're 'no good at telling jokes'. If you make yourself believe that (negative thinking – see Chapter 3) then, of course, it will become true. Nobody is good at telling jokes to begin with. But as with everything else, the more you do it the better you'll get. Apropos of which, here's a little joke:

A new girl is spending her first night in the dormitory. From a nearby bed a fellow pupil calls out '16'. At which everyone laughs. Another girl calls out, '23'. Again there's laughter. The new girl asks her neighbour to explain. It turns out the girls have allotted numbers to jokes so they can tell them quickly and not get caught for talking after lights out. The new girl decides to have a go. '11,' she calls out. No reaction. 'Four.' Still nothing. '16 again.' Still nothing. She turns to her neighbour. 'What's the problem?' And her neighbour explains, 'I'm afraid it's the way you tell them.'

Insight

Nerves kill even the best jokes. But don't worry, there are plenty more where they came from. So just keep telling them, because the more you do it, the less nervous you'll eventually be. If you don't feel that formal jokes suit you, you can simply cannibalize bits to decorate your normal conversation.

Keep smiling

Try slipping these into your next chat:

▶ *Just because I'm paranoid doesn't mean people aren't out to get me.*
▶ *You know, I used to think I was indecisive but now I'm not sure.*

Now, as to playfulness, there are three rules:

1 *Nothing cruel.*
2 *Nothing dangerous.*
3 *The other person has got to enjoy it just as much as you do.*

What most people call practical jokes usually aren't jokes at all. They're more like torture. That's not funny.

The aim of playfulness is that everybody has a good laugh. Think more in terms of simply being a little bit bolder than usual and using your imagination to create some audacious fun.

For example:

▶ *Make it a rule that when anybody in the household does something 'wrong' they have to pay a forfeit, such as sounding a hooter; when they do something 'right' they can ring a bell.*
▶ *From time to time, get a T-shirt printed with a funny message; wear it under a jacket or cardigan and then, at an appropriate moment, reveal it. (T-shirt messages work particularly well when you go to meet someone at an airport.)*
▶ *On hot, sunny days in the garden:*
  ▷ *Squirt someone with a water pistol; then hand out water pistols all round.*
  ▷ *Take out a tray of cold drink cans (having secretly given them a good shake beforehand).*
  ▷ *Create 'custard pies' using aerosol cream on circles of cardboard.*
▶ *If you live near the coast, on sultry nights take your partner for a drive, park at the beach and dare them to go skinny dipping with you.*

Great practical jokes

These classics from the annals of practical jokes might give you some inspiration. Note that nobody got hurt.

▶ *The film director John Huston once flew over a golf course during a tournament and dropped thousands of ping-pong balls.*

▶ *The actors David Niven and Errol Flynn shared a house together where, it was reputed, wild things went on. A guest arriving for a party was met by a butler and asked to leave his clothes in the hall, which he eagerly did, only to enter the lounge and find everyone else in evening dress.*

▶ *Students of Yale disguised themselves in Harvard colours and infiltrated themselves among the Harvard supporters at a football game in 2004. They handed out squares of red card and white card in accordance with a sequence they'd previously worked out. The Harvard students were told that when they held the cards up they'd spell out 'Go Harvard' in red lettering on a white background. They did as instructed and actually spelled 'We suck'.*

▶ *A chimpanzee called Tiao was nominated as mayor of Rio de Janeiro in 1988 and got over 400,000 votes. In the USA, a beer-drinking goat named Clay Henry III actually did become mayor of Lajitas, Texas and a black labrador became mayor of Rabbit Hash, Kentucky.*

For his birthday I bought my brother-in-law a diving mask, snorkel and flippers and told him I was going to take him to a little cove where there was plenty to see. When we swam around the headland he wasn't disappointed because I'd deliberately chosen a cove I knew was popular with nudists. He was quite embarrassed when his head first popped up out of the water, but we've had plenty of laughs about it since.

EVEN ANIMALS ENJOY A GOOD LAUGH

According to some researchers, chimpanzees, gorillas and orang-utans can laugh – a mixture of inhalations and exhalations – while dogs have a kind of panting laugh. A sort of chirping laugh has even been identified in rats. I keep ponies and although I've never seen them laugh, I've certainly seen them play practical jokes on one another. A favourite is that when one is busy eating all the others go off and hide.

> ## Try this
> Make a point of reading and watching something funny every day and of listening to some cheerful, energizing music every day.

10 THINGS TO REMEMBER

1 *Get to those negative emotions early; don't let them fester, grow and spoil your life. Remember that negative emotions make you ill – be happy, stay healthy.*

2 *The principal antidote to negative emotions is empathy, which means 'sending' your mind into another person.*

3 *Every force creates an equal and opposite force – so don't use force. When you give in to anger you build an 'angry brain', so if you must let your anger out, do it as laughter.*

4 *If the negative emotions concern someone else, discuss the problem as soon as possible and resolve it. Remember that it's better to be happy than to be revengeful.*

5 *Always start with the attitude that other people are reasonable and must have a valid reason for their behaviour. So, you'll be better off finding things to agree with, rather than to disagree with – being calm and reasonable isn't weakness but strength.*

6 *Don't cut off your nose to spite your face.*

7 *Feelings of guilt can paralyse all your emotions.*

8 *Failure is a very good teacher – don't be afraid of it.*

9 *Don't be hard on others; don't be hard on yourself.*

10 *Learn to tell jokes, be playful and laugh even when you don't feel like laughing – it's good practice and not being able to laugh is a disability just like any other.*

HOW HAPPY ARE YOU NOW?

Imagine that someone has said something you'd normally consider to be unfairly critical or even insulting. Will you get angry?

   a *Yes.*
   b *No.*

If you answered '(a)' to this (and the other two questions on this page) then move on to Chapter 5. But if you answered '(b)' because you're still flying into a temper, go back and read the beginning of this chapter. Do your best to discuss your feelings as quickly as possible. Men tend to be quite bad at that, thinking it's more masculine to appear unperturbed, but then fuming inwardly. Learn to say things like, 'I'm disappointed' or, 'I'm upset by what you've said' or, 'I think that's unfair' or, 'I need to talk about this'.

Have you forgiven anybody yet?

   a *Yes.*
   b *No.*

If you answered '(a)' to this (and the other two questions on this page) then move on to Chapter 5. If you answered '(b)' let's put that right immediately. Start with an easy one. Take someone whose perceived slight is often in your thoughts but not too serious. Now make the decision to forgive him or her. That doesn't mean you have to be great friends or even friends at all. It just means you're no longer going to keep that grievance on your 'scoreboard' and let it bother you. If you're finding it difficult, try a little harder to enter into the mind of that other person. See the situation from his or her point of view. If you're still finding it difficult, try to think of the other person as a child – adults often do act in childish ways.

Have you had a laugh today?

   a *Yes.*
   b *No.*

If you answered '(a)' to this (and the other two questions on this page) then move on to Chapter 5. But if you haven't actually had a laugh so far today, then you'd better do something about it *immediately*. Watch a funny film, read a funny book or swap jokes with someone. Otherwise just laugh anyway. Laughing exercise is as important as physical and mental exercise. Get practising.

Keep smiling

Take a lesson from the weather. It pays no attention to criticism.

5

Eating happiness

In this chapter you will learn:
- *how the food you eat can help make you happy*
- *why you should avoid 'empty calories'*
- *which foods have the happiest effect.*

> *Let food be your medicine.*
>
> Hippocrates (c. 460–c. 377 bce), Greek physician

> *By the proper intake of vitamins and other nutrients... the fraction of one's life during which one is happy becomes greater.*
>
> Linus Pauling (1901–94), double Nobel Prize winner

It may be difficult for people to describe happiness in words, but scientists can more or less define it in terms of hormones. Hormones are the chemical messengers in the body that tell other chemicals what to do. One of the most important hormones for happiness is serotonin. Without enough serotonin we feel anxious and even aggressive. With the optimum serotonin we feel calm and contented.

But where do these hormones come from? Ultimately, they come from food, which provides the raw materials. In a manner of speaking, you can actually eat happiness. And, in the same way, you can eat unhappiness.

A healthy diet is a happy diet

The word 'vitamin' has only been in use for a hundred years.
Which just goes to show how young the science of nutrition still is.
We know a lot more than we did, but there's a long way to go. It's
all incredibly complex.

Take tryptophan, for example. Tryptophan is the precursor for
serotonin. So it would seem to be a good idea to eat plenty of foods
containing tryptophan. And so it is – up to a point. But get too much
serotonin and, among other things, you'll find it extremely difficult
to have an orgasm. Which just might make you very, very *un*happy.

To complicate matters, tryptophan wouldn't have any effect if there
weren't certain other nutrients present. You need to package it along
with complex carbohydrates, vitamin B6, folic acid, magnesium and,
quite possibly, other substances that haven't even been discovered
yet. So you can see how testing tryptophan – or any substance – in
isolation might lead to a completely wrong conclusion.

Yet another complication is that the body has mechanisms for keeping
itself in balance. If it didn't, you'd undergo a personality change with
every meal. And to prevent the brain being damaged by poisons
there's a so-called 'blood-brain barrier', like a ring of hefty bouncers
to stop anything other than 'VIP chemicals' from getting through.

On top of all that, the brain has different systems for happiness and
unhappiness. They can work alone, together or against one another.
A chemical can have one effect in one part of the brain and a quite
different effect in another part of the brain. Pleasure and pain can
exist at the same time. Happiness and unhappiness are not direct
opposites.

It's because of this sort of complexity that a scientist sometimes
announces the nutritional secret of, say, long life or, indeed,
happiness, only to have the research overturned a few years later.

But this is what we think we know now.

Hormones, food and happiness

Hormones, including happiness hormones, come from amino acids. Some of these amino acids can be made by the body, so there doesn't seem to be much benefit in loading up on them in your diet, unless you're actually deficient. But others can't be made. They have to come from food, and tryptophan is one of them.

For adults the full list of amino acids that have to be eaten is:

- *isoleucine*
- *leucine*
- *lysine*
- *methionine*
- *phenylalanine*
- *threonine*
- *tryptophan*
- *valine.*

Although nowadays we have access to an enormous variety of foods, it's quite possible that we consume fewer essential nutrients than our ancestors. That's partly because so many nutrients have been stripped out during food processing and partly because we've switched to the wrong kinds of foods. A 7 kg (15 lb) monkey, for example, takes in around 600 mg (milligrams) of vitamin C per day and 4,500 mg of calcium. Broadly speaking, kilo for kilo, that's 100 times as much vitamin C and calcium as is generally thought to be essential for human beings.

OK, monkeys aren't people. But quite a few scientists, including the late double-Nobel Prize winner Linus Pauling, have concluded precisely that the generally accepted healthy vitamin intake is far too low. He believed human consumption of vitamin C should be increased at least 20 and possibly as much as 300 times. He also had similar ideas for vitamins A, E and the B group.

There is a logic behind it all. Human beings evolved on a 'Stone Age' diet of fruits, vegetables, nuts and seeds along with a small quantity of fish and lean meat. Today's diet for most people is very, very different.

Here are some of the key chemicals that are connected with food:

- *Dopamine is the neurotransmitter that makes you seek pleasure and enjoy life. It produces enthusiasm, exuberance and joy. It creates anticipation and motivation. Without it you wouldn't ever do anything. When you have a pleasurable experience, dopamine reinforces it and makes you want it again (so it's also associated with addiction). Dopamine is synthesized from tyrosine, an amino acid particularly found in wheatgerm and milk.*

- *Endorphins are the body's own natural painkiller or opioid, named from the words 'endogenous' (meaning 'within the body') and 'morphine'. Like actual morphine, endorphins can create euphoria. The body can be 'tricked' into releasing endorphins by spices hot enough to 'burn' the tongue.*

- *Noradrenaline (norepinephrine) is synthesized from tyrosine. Although it's also associated with stress, in the right circumstances noradrenaline elevates mood.*

- *Oxytocin – among other things, this hormone promotes touching and affectionate behaviour, which tends to make people happy. It's lowered by alcohol.*

- *PEA (phenylethylamine) is the amphetamine-like substance that produces that 'walking on air' feeling, especially when you're in love. It is found in chocolate and some soft drinks (but there's doubt as to how well it can be absorbed from them) and is produced during vigorous exercise.*

- *Serotonin is a neurotransmitter that makes you feel peaceful, unaggressive, monogamous and content. But it reduces sex drive and the speed of orgasm and too much can make you sleepy and lethargic. As we've seen, it's synthesized from tryptophan.*

> *Testosterone is considered the 'male' sex hormone but it is*
> *also present in women at lower levels. It increases sex drive,*
> *but too much causes aggression and irritability. Eating meat*
> *increases testosterone; veganism lowers it.*

Insight

None of these qualities are absolutes. They can be moderated
by other hormones and chemicals and a lot depends on
dose and personal response. You might, for example, decide
to eat more meat for the positive get-up-and-go effects of
testosterone, but end up irritable and unhappy.

The principles of happy eating

Illness is a pretty common cause of unhappiness, and poor diet is
a pretty common cause of illness. The general principle of healthy
eating is this: you can only eat so much in a day, so make sure it's
nutritious.

In other words, there are 'empty calories' that contain very few
vitamins and minerals (sweets, crisps, 'junk food') and, on the
other hand, there are calories that come packed together with
vitamins and minerals. So do your best to restrict those empty
calories. In order to make sure you're getting enough of the
nutrients for health and happiness, your diet each day should
include the following (a cup is 250ml):

> *whole grains, such as rice, barley and wholemeal bread,*
> *as the foundation of at least one meal*
> *vegetables, including green leafy vegetables (about four cups)*
> *fruit (about four cups)*
> *nuts, seeds and legumes (about one cup).*

You also need to pay particular attention to the kind of fat
in your diet.

Minimize:

- *trans-fatty acids – which are in lamb, beef, dairy products and margarine (which means cakes and biscuits as well)*
- *saturated fats – which are mostly in animal products*
- *omega-6 polyunsaturated fatty acids (PUFAs) – which are found in animal products and vegetable oils.*

Maximize:

- *monounsaturated fats such as olive oil*
- *omega-3 polyunsaturated fatty acids (PUFAs) found in oily fish, rapeseed (canola), soy, walnut and flaxseed oils.*

About two-thirds of the human brain by weight and about 75 per cent of the myelin sheath that surrounds nerves is made up of polyunsaturated fatty acids. The key difference between omega-6s and omega-3s is this:

- *Omega-6s cause inflammation, constrict blood vessels, encourage blood platelets to stick together, form rigid cell membranes and release free radicals which destroy cells.*
- *Omega-3s reduce inflammation, dilate blood vessels, deter blood platelets from sticking together and form flexible cell membranes.*

For optimum brain functioning, including happiness, you want flexible cell membranes, that is, omega-3s. But in the modern diet, omega-6s tend to outweigh omega-3s ten times over. Although omega-6s are essential, this ratio is bad. What you actually need to do is to aim for more omega-3s than omega-6s.

Insight

Flaxseed is the only known non-fish oil that provides more omega-3s than omega-6s. In other words, if you don't eat fish, try to use flaxseed oil as often as possible. When you can't use flaxseed oil, use olive oil, which is only 8 per cent omega-6.

Food allergies can make you depressed

Food allergies are sometimes a cause of low moods and even depression. The most frequent culprits are:

- ▶ *citrus fruits*
- ▶ *coffee*
- ▶ *dairy products*
- ▶ *gluten (a protein found in wheat, rye, oats and barley)*
- ▶ *nuts*
- ▶ *soya*
- ▶ *tea.*

Stress (a bad thing in so many other ways, too) can be responsible for letting nutrients into the bloodstream before complete digestion. These can then go on to cause allergies. If you develop allergies for no obvious reason, think back and see if stress could be the cause.

TREATMENT

Try eliminating all suspect foods from your diet and then re-introducing them one at a time. (But don't do this if your allergy is severe because it could cause the reaction to be dangerously intense next time.) If you can't readily identify the allergen, enlist the help of your doctor.

Tip
Antihistamines are the standard way of reducing and shortening allergic reactions, but they often cause drowsiness. As an alternative, ask your doctor about vitamin C which has mild antihistamine properties.

Your A–Z guide to happy food and drink

Healthy nutrition is a whole book in itself. Here we'll just concentrate on foods and nutrients that are directly associated with happiness. As we'll see, some essential 'happy' nutrients are often lacking in the modern diet.

ALCOHOL

Alcohol is at the top of the list not because it's the best but simply because it begins with the first letter of the alphabet. It's impossible to ignore a substance that most people associate with 'having a good time' – but too much is catastrophic.

How does it work?
Alcohol indirectly increases the feel-good chemical dopamine by inhibiting it from being broken down in the brain.

What dose?
About a glass of wine a day with the evening meal would be about right. Regularly drinking more only diminishes the effect, creating a tolerance that requires increasing amounts of alcohol to achieve the same mood enhancement. The 'official' safe maximum is considered to be 21 units a week (and not more than four units in any one day) for a man, and 14 units a week (and not more than three units in any one day) for a woman. However, according to Carole L. Hart, who led a team of researchers at the University of Glasgow, the threshold at which negative effects outweigh positive effects is much lower, at just 11 units a week for a man.

Any side effects?
Plenty. Some people keep increasing the dose to overcome their tolerance and end up addicted. Dopamine has the interesting ability to link with whatever visual image you're looking at when the chemical hits you. In other words, the very sight of alcohol can set off an addict's synapses. Addiction can lead to dementia, psychosis, liver damage, depression – the very opposite of the intended effect – and even suicide. Alcohol also reduces oxytocin, the chemical that makes you feel like cuddling.

Keep smiling

A man went to the doctor because his hands were trembling. The doctor asked him: 'Do you drink much?'

'Hardly at all,' said the patient. 'I spill most of it.'

BRAZIL NUTS

Brazilians are said to be among the happiest people in the world – maybe the nut is the secret.

How does it work?

Brazil nuts contain more selenium than any other food and about 2,500 times more selenium than any other nut. Selenium deficiency causes low moods and depression.

What dose?

In one study of men and women aged between 14 and 74, those given 100 mcg (micrograms) of selenium a day were more upbeat than controls who received a placebo. The average Briton eats under 50 mcg a day. A couple of freshly shelled nuts or half a dozen ready-shelled will bring you up to your daily requirement.

Any side effects?

Selenium is actually toxic in large amounts so don't exceed the recommended 'dose' of Brazils. A fungus that can grow on the nuts is carcinogenic. Brazils imported into Europe are carefully screened but, for safety, don't eat any that are yellow inside – the correct colour is pale ivory.

CAFFEINE

Caffeine is a psychoactive drug that can boost mood and increase mental energy. It's very important to stress the word 'can' because it all depends on the dose and on an individual's make up.

How does it work?
It would seem that caffeine resembles the structure of a brain chemical called adenosine. Adenosine's role is to dampen down activity, but caffeine has the ability to displace it from the nerve cell receptor sites so the adenosine can't do its job and the brain remains more alert.

What dose?
Even a very tiny dose of caffeine has an effect and it lasts for several hours. Experts say the optimum dose is around 100–200 mg in the morning and the same again in the late afternoon when energy levels often slump.

As the following table shows, the most potent source of caffeine is fresh, filtered coffee. One cup (5 fl oz/140 mg) is all it takes. If you drink instant coffee or tea you'll need two cups a time to equal this dose. Despite their famed kick, energy drinks generally lag behind at around half the strength of filter coffee (but it's easier to drink more). There's also caffeine in chocolate, but the amount in a cocoa drink is negligible. You'll get more in a bar of plain chocolate but, even so, you'd have to consume your entire day's allowance of calories to get the optimum.

Sources of caffeine	mg
Cup of filter coffee	115
Cup of percolated coffee	80
Cup of instant coffee	65
Cup of tea (bags or leaves)	60
Glass of cola or energy drink	44
Cup of instant tea	30
1 oz/30 g of plain chocolate	20
1 oz/30 g of milk chocolate	6
Cup of hot chocolate	4

Any side effects?
Some studies have found that coffee can increase the risk of heart disease and this appears to be the case even if it's decaffeinated. On that basis, tea would appear to be a safer source of caffeine, especially as tea fights certain cancers and viruses and acts as an anticoagulant.

Large doses of caffeine can have the opposite of the desired effect, causing anxiety. In susceptible individuals, even one or two cups can cause panic attacks. If you have these problems, it would be a good idea to cut out coffee altogether.

Which brings us to another side effect. Coffee is addictive. Fine if you can always get it when you want. But the first day you can't you'll be lethargic and even depressed.

CHILLI PEPPERS

Chilli peppers probably aren't the sort of thing you'd want to eat every day but, now and then, they're a fun way of giving yourself a happiness boost.

How does it work?
Chilli peppers contain capsaicin, the chemical responsible for the burning sensation. But capsaicin is also a painkiller. When inhaled it stops headaches and when it's injected it reduces joint pain. It seems that when you eat hot chilli peppers, the burning sensation causes messages to be sent to the brain, which responds by releasing endorphins, the body's natural painkillers. With each additional pepper you get an additional rush.

What dose?
If you're not used to hot food start out with small doses and build up.

Any side effects?
Chilli peppers clear the sinuses, act as a decongestant and keep the blood mobile.

CHOCOLATE

Many people instinctively reach for the chocolate when they feel down, and with good reason. But it's important to choose a variety that's at least 60 per cent cocoa, the ingredient that contains all the mood-boosting chemicals. Milk chocolate just won't do.

How does it work?
Cocoa is a veritable cocktail of happy chemicals:

- *caffeine (see above)*
- *theobromine – a mild stimulant that may produce arousal and a feeling of wellbeing*
- *phenylethylamine (PEA) – chocolate undoubtedly contains this amphetamine-like compound but its absorption from chocolate hasn't been proven*
- *anandamide-boosting chemicals – anandamide binds to specific receptors in the brain, heightening sensation and increasing pleasure*
- *1MeTIQ, a chemical that might inhibit Parkinson's disease*
- *antioxidants, which may prevent free radical damage to the brain*
- *procyanidins, which act as both antioxidants and anti-inflammatories; they also relax smooth muscles, which can aid erection during sex.*

What dose?
There's no known optimum dose, but something like 1 oz/30 g a day would be reasonable.

Any side effects?
Dark chocolate contains around 600 calories per 3.5 oz/100 g, so you'll put on weight if you eat too much.

COMPLEX CARBOHYDRATES

The brain is fuelled by glucose, but eating sugar isn't the best way of providing it. Eating sugar leads to highs and lows (as well

as various health problems). What the brain needs most of all is a
steady supply and that comes best from complex carbohydrates,
which break down slowly and release energy constantly. Complex
carbohydrates include dried beans, pasta, vegetables, cereals and
bread.

How does it work?
Complex carbohydrates are happiness foods because they facilitate
the production of serotonin.

What dose?
You need about 1 oz/30 g of pure carbohydrate in order to feel
more tranquil. In a day, aim to get at least half your calories from
complex carbohydrates (most people don't).

Any side effects?
Endurance athletes load up on complex carbohydrates to provide
their muscles with the glycogen they need. But carbohydrates don't
work well for everybody – some people just feel lethargic after
eating, rather than content.

FOLIC ACID (FOLATE)

Folic acid, a B vitamin, occurs naturally in green leafy vegetables
and legumes, but most people don't get enough.

How does it work?
Folic acid deficiency causes serotonin levels to plummet.

What dose?
The generally recommended level is 300–400 mcg, but
most people get around 200 mcg – equivalent to 5 oz/140 g
of cooked spinach. Either eat more vegetables or take a
supplement.

Any side effects?
Folic acid can mask vitamin B12 deficiency. At very high doses
folic acid can be toxic.

GARLIC

Researchers at the University of Hanover, testing the effect of garlic on high cholesterol, came up with a finding they hadn't been expecting. Garlic boosts mood and reduces anxiety, irritability and fatigue.

How does it work?
Nobody knows at the moment, but garlic is packed with interesting chemicals, notably allicin which is responsible for the smell.

What dose?
One to two raw cloves a day.

Any side effects?
The smell. But that goes away with regular use. Garlic also boosts the immune system, fights cancer and is an antibiotic, blood thinner, expectorant and decongestant. Oh yes, and it really does help men have sex – which tends to make them cheerful.

OATS

The traditional Scottish breakfast has almost magical properties.

How does it work?
Oats contain tryptophan, the precursor for serotonin, as well as B vitamins, calcium, magnesium and potassium, all of which are essential for healthy nerves.

What dose?
About a bowl a day would be good.

Any side effects?
Half a cup of oat bran or a whole cup of dry oatmeal will lower undesirable LDL cholesterol by about 20 per cent while raising beneficial HDL cholesterol by around 15 per cent. Oats also have anti-cancer properties.

WHEATGERM

Wheatgerm is the highly nutritious part of the wheat grain that is normally removed during milling. But it will still be present in wholemeal bread and can also be bought separately.

How does it work?
Wheatgerm contains tyrosine, a precursor for dopamine. Tyrosine can be made in the body, but it certainly doesn't do any harm to guarantee supplies. Wheatgerm also contains the raw ingredients for noradrenaline (norepinephrine) and serotonin.

What dose?
Realistically, it would be difficult to eat more than about 1 oz/30 g sprinkled on food or as part of wholemeal bread, but it would be considered a useful quantity.

Any side effects?
Wheatgerm can make an important contribution to your daily requirement for magnesium, vitamin B6, folic acid and zinc.

ZINC

A deficiency of zinc is associated with poor memory, slow response and depression.

How does it work?
Zinc can rejuvenate the thymus gland, an important part of the immune system, is an antioxidant that can work in the brain, plays an important role in memory, and boosts testosterone, which can make you feel more dynamic.

What dose?
Opinions vary, but most authorities favour 10–15 mg of zinc per day. On that basis, most people are on the margin or deficient, especially as less than half the zinc in food is absorbed.
Only oysters are sufficiently rich in zinc to guarantee an adequate intake. If you don't eat oysters take a supplement.

Any side effects?
Zinc can perk up the sex life of men who are deficient.

> **Insight**
>
> The 'happy diet' is nothing at all like a slimming diet, so you shouldn't have any problem sticking to it. In itself it will neither cause you to lose weight nor put it on. Its only function is to help you be more happy. You don't have to cut out carbohydrates, you can drink in moderation and you can even eat chocolate. So there's really nothing to stop you.

10 THINGS TO REMEMBER

1 Hormones are chemical messengers that, among other things, can 'tell' us to be happy.

2 The raw materials for hormones are amino acids.

3 Some amino acids can be created in the body, but others have to be consumed in food.

4 Today's diet is lacking in some of the essential nutrients for happiness.

5 Don't eat 'empty calories' – that is, foods with minimal amounts of vitamins and minerals.

6 Try to eat more omega-3s than omega-6s.

7 Food allergies can cause low moods and depression.

8 About a glass of wine with dinner is the optimum amount of alcohol.

9 Happy foods include Brazil nuts, chilli peppers, chocolate, coffee, complex carbohydrates, garlic, oats, tea and wheatgerm.

10 Happy food supplements include folic acid (folate), selenium and zinc.

HOW HAPPY ARE YOU NOW?

Is the 'happy diet' working?

a *Yes.*
b *I'm following it but I haven't noticed any difference.*
c *I'm not following it.*

If you answered '(a)' you're ready to move on to Chapter 6.
If you answered '(b)', well, changes in diet take time to produce
results. So keep on with the 'happy diet' and also move to
Chapter 6. If you're not yet following it, read through the chapter
again. You'll see that the 'happy diet' is a lot easier than a
slimming diet. For a start, you don't have to give up carbohydrates,
you can drink a little alcohol and a sensible amount of chocolate is
actually recommended. So there's really no reason not to try it.

Keep smiling

Chocolate is better than a relationship because:

► Chocolate never snores.
► With chocolate there's no need to fake enjoyment.
► You're never too old for chocolate.
► You can have chocolate whenever you want.

6

Inner happiness

In this chapter you will learn:
- *how you can experience happiness through meditation*
- *what meditation feels like and how to do it*
- *how meditation can help you be happier in your everyday life.*

What lies behind us and what lies before us are tiny matters, compared with what lies within us.

Henry Stanley Hoskins (1875–1965), American writer

In shallow souls, even the fish of small things can cause a commotion. In oceanic minds, the largest fish makes hardly a ripple.

Hindu proverb

There's a profound state of inner happiness that's available to all of us. But, unlike 'ordinary' happiness, it's not something we can create at any given moment. Rather, think of it more like a reservoir we can *access*. We only have to know how to get at it.

Meditation is one of the ways of accessing this inner happiness. Don't go thinking that meditation is some kind of Oriental, quasi-religious mumbo-jumbo that has no relevance to your everyday life in the West. In one way or another we all meditate at times. In this chapter we're going to take things a little further and learn how to meditate more profoundly. We're going to learn how to drink from the reservoir.

So start meditating. Or, to put it another way: don't just do something – sit there!

How could it be possible that sitting cross-legged and thinking about nothing very much at all could have even a remote impact on happiness? When you put it like that it doesn't sound very likely. Yet the evidence is there. People who meditate regularly say they feel happier, scientists can measure the increase in 'happy chemicals' and several physical indicators of wellbeing also improve. Researchers have monitored the brains of people who begin meditating and found that, over a period of months, activity tends to increase in the frontal lobe of the left brain. That's the part associated with higher moods and optimism.

You might access your inner happiness in your very first session, but it takes most people a few weeks. Thereafter, meditation deepens until, perhaps after a year or two, something very profound is experienced. Almost everyone talks of feeling calmer and more peaceful. Accompanying these feelings are those of patience and compassion. Later come feelings of intense joy. And all this, in turn, leads to a more positive engagement with life.

In fact, it isn't necessary to sit cross-legged. And 'thinking about nothing' is only one of several approaches. As we'll see in a moment, there are various different styles of meditation.

Raymond's story

Raymond took up yoga about seven years ago and began meditating three years ago. For the first two years, he says, he meditated purely for the discipline. It was only in the third year that he began to experience 'strange' things. When you meet him he has a look in his eyes, which suggests some special knowledge.

'I now look forward to this part of the day,' he says. 'I sometimes can hardly wait for it. It's the time when I'm alone with myself and completely in the present. I feel a connection with everything. It makes me very happy.'

So what is meditation?

Meditation is, firstly, a way of trying to get control of your mind. When unpleasant and worrying thoughts pop up in your head uninvited you'll be able to get rid of them. On the other hand, when you want to summon up positive emotions and happy thoughts – when you want to draw on the reservoir – you'll have the ability.

In the dictionary, the word 'meditation' can be used simply to mean concentrated thinking or serious reflection. But here we're concerned with meditation as an altered state of consciousness involving one or more of the following:

- *freeing the mind of all thoughts and just 'being'*
- *focusing on the present moment*
- *focusing on a single issue*
- *integrating the subconscious with the conscious.*

More technically, meditation means entering a state of consciousness that is neither the normal, everyday state of being awake, nor the state of being asleep. There are four categories of brain waves:

- *Beta – 13–40 Hz, the fastest frequencies, associated with normal waking consciousness and being alert.*
- *Alpha – 7–13 Hz, the next-fastest frequencies, associated with feeling relaxed, daydreaming, reverie and light meditation.*
- *Theta – 4–7 Hz, slower again, associated with dreaming sleep and deep meditation.*
- *Delta – under 4 Hz, the slowest, associated with deep sleep.*

What's the point? After all, we all sleep several hours a night in the theta and delta states so what difference does another 20 minutes or so of meditation make? In fact, the sleeping state is quite different from the meditative state.

When you go into the space of nothingness, everything becomes known.

Buddha (c.563–483 bce), religious leader

Insight

Notice the use of the word 'associated' because, in fact, it's possible for two or three or even four frequencies to be present at the same time. Although 'light' meditation is normally said to be in alpha mode and 'deep' meditation in theta mode, in practice deep meditation can involve not just alpha but also beta and theta and, in rare cases, all four. That is normally the preserve of a 'master', possessing what some call 'the awakened mind'. But everyone who meditates will combine frequencies in a way that is different from sleeping.

So the point of meditation is:

▶ *to experience inner happiness.*

And it could also be:

▶ *to refresh and revitalize yourself after your day's work*
▶ *to forget, for a while, your cares about the past and your worries for the future*
▶ *to try to understand the nature of the mind*
▶ *to increase your control over your mind*
▶ *to cultivate a calmer mind and a more tranquil outlook*
▶ *to develop a more balanced mental state in respect of a particular issue*
▶ *to gain a greater understanding of your true nature*
▶ *to become more totally aware.*

PHYSICAL BENEFITS OF MEDITATION

Meditation isn't only good for the mind. It can lower blood pressure and improve both the cardiovascular and immune functions as well.

Keep smiling

Q: How many contemplative monks does it take to change a light bulb?

A: Three. One to change the light bulb. One to not change the light bulb. One to neither change nor not change the light bulb.

Keep smiling

Sign outside a yoga school: Yoga teacher needed – enquire within.

How to meditate

TIME OF DAY

You can meditate at any time. Some teachers recommend first thing in the morning, especially before dawn, as a way of setting you up for the day. Others recommend the late evening, when everything has been done, as a way of unwinding from the day. Still others like to take advantage of the natural tendency to feel sleepy around the end of the working day. But be careful. Sleeping and meditation are different things and although it's easier to get into a meditative state when your body and mind have slowed down of their own accord there's always the danger of snoozing rather than meditating.

Insight

Find out what works best for you and then try to stick to it. Your body and mind will adapt accordingly and you'll find it increasingly easy to get into a meditative state at the same time every day.

WHERE TO MEDITATE

You can meditate anywhere. But most people like to have a special place and some also like to have special 'props' to help them get into the meditative state.

As a beginner you're probably best to have a quiet place where you won't be disturbed. Except for open-eyed styles of meditation, it will help if the room is dim or even dark. You could wear an eye mask. Make it a nice place so that you look forward to going to it and come to associate it with meditation.

Keep smiling

Mahatma Gandhi was asked what he thought of Western civilization. He replied: 'I think it would be a good idea.'

THE POSITION

The pose traditionally associated with meditation is the lotus position. That's to say, sitting on the floor with the right foot on the left thigh and the left foot on the right thigh, so that the left ankle crosses over on top of the right ankle. The idea behind it is that it's extremely stable so that, in deep meditation, you won't topple over; at the same time, it's not a position in which it's easy to fall asleep.

Fortunately, the lotus position is not essential, which is just as well because very few people can manage it at all, let alone for a whole session of meditation. When you meditate you need to be comfortable. That's vital. You don't want to be distracted by thinking how painful your ankles or knees are.

If you can easily do the half-lotus (only one foot resting on the opposite thigh, the other foot going under the opposite thigh) this is all well and good. If not, just sit cross-legged. In whichever of these poses you sit it's important that you keep your spine straight.

Rest your hands on your knees. One way to do this is with the palms up and the thumb and forefinger of each hand touching to form an 'O'. But there are other ways, as you'll see in the rest of this chapter.

There are two alternatives to sitting on the floor. The lotus-type position comes down to us from an era when furniture hadn't been invented but, in fact, you can meditate perfectly well sitting on a dining chair or even an office swivel chair. The key element is to sit away from the back of the chair, keeping a straight spine. Just place your hands, palms down, lightly on your knees.

The other alternative is to lie down. Many teachers frown on this as not being 'proper' and because of the danger of falling asleep. But, in fact, it's an excellent position for meditating because it automatically reduces beta waves. As with the other positions, the spine should be straight, so lie on your back with your arms by your sides, palms up, and your feet shoulder width apart. To overcome the danger of falling asleep, try lying on the floor rather than the bed so you don't get too comfortable.

HOW LONG SHOULD I MEDITATE FOR?

You could meditate all day. But, in the context of a busy modern life 20–30 minutes is the sort of time to aim for. The longer you can devote to it the more likely you are to reach a deep state. Nevertheless, even a minute's meditation is better than nothing. And sometimes it's possible to experience a meditative state while doing other things, such as walking or running.

However long the session, the benefits ripple out far beyond it. It's just the same as when, for example, something happens to make you angry. The incident might last no more than a few seconds but it could be hours before you feel calm again. So it is with the positive effects of meditation.

Insight

Some people like to set a timer. This can work well because it removes any anxiety about not meditating for long enough or, on the other hand, taking too long and being late for the next thing you have to do. But others prefer to let whatever happens happen.

Meditating for happiness

So you're sitting or lying down. Then what? Different people use different techniques and again you need to experiment to find out what works best for you. Some people, for example, stare at a candle flame or an image or a wall, others repeat mantras, still others repeat small almost imperceptible gestures.

Here's a simple way of meditating for happiness.

1 *Sitting or lying down with your eyes closed, notice your breathing.*
2 *Without forcing anything, gradually slow down your breathing.*
3 *Make your exhalations longer than your inhalations.*
4 *Empty your mind of any thoughts of past or future.*
5 *Just concentrate on experiencing the present moment, which is your breath.*
6 *If any thoughts push their way into your mind just let them drift past; don't pursue them.*
7 *When your breathing is slow and relaxed, notice your heartbeat.*
8 *Without forcing anything, gradually try to think it slower.*

9 *Next notice the sound of your blood in your ears.*

10 *Without forcing anything, gradually try to think it slower.*

11 *In the same way, visit any other parts of your body that you choose.*

12 *Now notice the little dots that 'illuminate' the blackness of your closed eyes.*

13 *Imagine the dots are stars and that you're floating in an immense space inside your own body.*

14 *Relax your jaw and let your mouth open into a smile.*

15 *Continue like this as long as you like.*

Tips

If you can't seem to get into a meditative state at all, try lying on the floor rather than sitting.

Try touching the tip of your ring finger against the fleshy base of your thumb as you breathe in and moving it away as you breathe out. As you breathe in think 'so' and as you breathe out think 'hum' – it's a classic mantra.

Gradually slow down your breathing, making your exhalation longer than your inhalation.

Let your mouth fall open and your tongue relax completely and drop out.

AM I MEDITATING?

Beginners often wonder if they're meditating correctly or even at all. What should it feel like? In fact, there is no precise definition, but the stages of increasingly deeper and deeper meditation should go something like this:

▶ **Stage 1.** *Your mind is no longer filled with everyday matters and you sense that you're drifting towards sleep; you're on the very fringe of the meditative state.*

- ▶ **Stage 2.** *As you go deeper, images may come at you from nowhere. You don't actually fall asleep but start to feel as if you're floating. You may feel like rocking and swaying; that's fine at this stage but you'll need to stop moving to go deeper.*
- ▶ **Stage 3.** *You become intensely aware of the functioning of your body – breathing, heartbeat, blood flow – but at the same time you no longer know where your body ends and other things begin. Parts of your body may feel very heavy.*
- ▶ **Stage 4.** *You feel 'spaced out' and quite detached but, at the same time, alert.*
- ▶ **Stage 5.** *You feel in touch with the universe and nothing else matters at all.*

The deepest meditative states are usually only reached by those who have been practising for a long time – perhaps two or three years. But you may occasionally experience moments of those deeper states even as a beginner.

Insight

Remember that meditation is not a competition. Every experience of meditation is slightly different. Don't set out with a goal and then consider the session a failure because you didn't achieve it. Just experience and enjoy whatever occurs.

Maggie's story

I was sitting in the half lotus at the edge of a lake. It was a beautiful, sunny, autumn day in northern Spain with just the lightest of winds. In front of me there were some reeds. And as I moved into a deeper state of meditation I had the feeling I had become just like one of those reeds. I felt the warmth of the sun and the movement of the breeze and I heard the water lapping gently and the bees buzzing from flower to flower. I was almost overwhelmed by the dance of life and, like the reeds, I existed, but no more than that. I existed with no regrets, fears, hopes or desires.

CAN I LISTEN TO MUSIC?

Most music is distracting for meditation. Even if you're not consciously paying attention to it, it will sweep you away in its own rhythms. But non-melodic music is somewhat different. You may be able to find something suitably Oriental in the 'World Music' or 'New Age' categories. There definitely shouldn't be any recognizable tune. You might also like to try sound effects – waterfalls, streams, wind and so forth. If you do play something, play it very quietly.

It is only in the depths of silence that the voice of God can be heard.

Sai Baba (1838–1918), Indian guru

Meditating for practical benefits

Above we've looked at a direct experience of inner happiness. A different style of meditation can be used in a practical way to help you create more happiness in your everyday life.

This is closer to what we might call 'having a good think'. But it's very different from the normal approach to meditation. The biggest difference is that you're not looking for a solution to a problem. In fact, the desired outcome of your meditation is decided from the very beginning: to regain a calmer and more tranquil frame of mind regarding a difficult issue, and to become happier as a result.

In other words, you're not working out how you can get even, you're not working out how you can get your own way and you're certainly not sulking. You start out knowing that the solution is not to change something in the outside world, but to change something inside yourself. You meditate to find out what to change and how.

The heart has reasons that reason knows not of.

Blaise Pascal (1623–62), French philosopher

Let's take an example. Suppose a long-term relationship has ended and you have to sort out who gets what and who pays what. Unfortunately, your ex-partner is constantly angry, which makes you very upset and you tend to respond in the same angry way. No progress is being made.

This is how you might meditate on the problem, with the aim of preserving your own happiness. It's important to stress that getting the maximum amount of money is not the object of the exercise. The way forward is to empathize with your ex-partner, that is, to put yourself in the position of your ex-partner to see how it feels, so you can behave accordingly. Let's say you were the one who broke up the relationship.

▶ **Step 1.** *Get yourself into a meditative state, as described earlier.*
▶ **Step 2.** *Try to feel what your ex is feeling. It could be that he or she is thinking something like this: 'I've been rejected and that makes me feel a failure. I also feel, by turns, shocked, disorientated, upset, bitter, despondent and lacking in self-esteem. In order to build up my self-esteem I have to get the maximum from my ex. I'm using anger as a way of dominating the situation and getting what I want. It also helps blot out all the pain. It isn't at all easy feeling this way and when I get an angry response back, it only makes me worse. If I heard some words from my ex to indicate understanding and sympathy, if my ex would just make some concessions and be conciliatory, then I'd be willing to take a softer line.'*
▶ **Step 3.** *Visualize yourself talking together with your ex. Visualize saying different things. Which is the one that would best preserve your mental equilibrium? Given your new empathy with your ex, listen to the response your ex is likely to make to each of those different approaches.*
▶ **Step 4.** *Visualize how you're going to feel when your ex gives those responses. Again, which is the response from your ex that's least likely to damage your happiness? Analyse what it is that's stopping you from making the approach that will make you feel happy and, hopefully, elicit the desired response from your ex.*

▶ **Step 5.** *Visualize yourself changing your attitude to the situation and, instead, adopting an approach that will maximize happiness. Visualize yourself behaving in this new way and not allowing yourself to be deterred, no matter what response your ex actually gives.*

If you do this conscientiously, you'll see why getting angry isn't likely to produce the happiness you want. Step 5 is very important because when it comes to the reality, your ex may not behave in the way you'd prefer. If you've already rehearsed that in your meditation you'll be prepared for it. You'll be able to deal calmly with the situation and preserve the serenity of your mind.

Insight

It's important to repeat that the purpose of such a meditation is not how you can get your way or how you can get more, or anything like that. It's how you can change your way of looking at the situation so you can be more happy.

You can't teach anybody anything, only make them realize the answers are already inside them.

Galileo (1564–1642), Italian astronomer

Here are some other things you could meditate on:

▶ *the good things your partner does/did for you*
▶ *the things you can be grateful for*
▶ *anger and what it does to you*
▶ *the problems other people have in their lives*
▶ *the scale, grandeur and mystery of the universe.*

Tip

The Dalai Lama teaches several meditations for anger. One involves imagining someone you love who nevertheless becomes extremely angry with you. You can see that person's face contorted with rage and it isn't nice. Now imagine that the situation is reversed and it's you who has become angry. Do you really want to be like that?

Meditating on the day's events

This is a style of meditation that's very appropriate for last thing at night in bed. The idea is to review what happened and how you reacted, not in a self-critical way but in an optimistic, forward-looking sort of way. In other words, your thoughts might go something like this: 'I was a little bit brusque with someone at work; I'll put that right by making a point of being more pleasant tomorrow. I spent far too long trying to get something absolutely perfect; I now realize I wasted a lot of time so I won't do that again. My partner criticized something I'd done and instead of becoming annoyed, I looked at the situation from my partner's point of view, understood, and felt much better, which resulted in a lovely evening. Good.'

Where does inner happiness come from?

So far we've talked about accessing the reservoir of inner happiness, but I've said nothing about what feeds the reservoir, or how you can enlarge it. In fact, it's fed by your spiritual connection with everything else in the universe. If you don't believe that, you can nevertheless still gain tremendous benefit from meditating. So don't stop just because talk of 'spiritual' things puts you off. But if you are interested in the spiritual aspects of meditation, you'll find a lot more in Chapter 11.

10 THINGS TO REMEMBER

1 Inner happiness can't be created at any given moment but is accessed.

2 Meditation is one of the ways of accessing inner happiness.

3 Scientists have demonstrated that meditation increases activity in the frontal lobe of the left brain – the part associated with higher moods and optimism.

4 Meditation can give you control of your mind so unpleasant thoughts can't enter on their own.

5 Meditation can bring immediate benefits, but it can take as much as two years or more to reach the deepest states.

6 Meditation is an altered state of consciousness, which occasionally occurs in daily life, but normally requires focused attention.

7 There are four categories of brain waves; meditation is associated with alpha and theta states but can involve all four.

8 Meditation can benefit not only the mind but also the body, lowering blood pressure and boosting the immune system.

9 Meditation can be done any time, anywhere and in any position, but the meditative state is more easily achieved with regularity.

10 You can use the meditative state to help you find positive solutions to problems.

HOW HAPPY ARE YOU NOW?

Is meditation making you happier?

a *Yes.*
b *No, I'm too busy and stressed to meditate.*
c *No, I'm not doing it.*

If you answered '(a)' move on to Chapter 7. If you answered '(b)', reflect that feeling stressed is a very good reason to meditate. Admittedly, though, it can be much harder to get into the right frame of mind. Remember that meditating is *not* an indulgence but, among other things, can be a tool to make you more effective. Looked at like that, you can surely find 20 minutes a day in your schedule. If it's just a question of believing that meditation is mumbo-jumbo, well, at the very worst it's harmless, so what have you got to lose by trying it?

Keep smiling

First man: How's your son? Is he still unemployed?
Second man: Yes. But he's meditating now.
First man: What's that?
Second man: Don't know exactly. But at least it's better than sitting around doing nothing.

7

How to get happy-fit

In this chapter you will learn:
- *how exercise will make you happier*
- *how to assess your happy-fitness*
- *how to experience the 'runner's high'*
- *how to design a happy-fit programme*
- *how to stay motivated.*

> *Running should be viewed as a wonder drug, analogous to penicillin, morphine and the tricyclics... Physical activity is positively associated with good mental health, especially positive mood, general wellbeing and less anxiety and depression.*

> William Morgan, PhD (past president American Psychological Association Division of Exercise and Sport Psychology)

Let's get one thing clear right at the start. Contrary to everything you may have believed, exercise makes you happy. Exercise is fun. Yes, fun – F U N. There's no surer way to boost your mood both immediately and in the longer term.

You may already know it. But if you don't, I'm going to try to convince you. Scientists can measure these things. And they've found that the levels of endorphins, phenylethylamine and noradrenaline/norepinephrine – some of what might be called 'happy chemicals' – shoot up when you exercise.

We've already met noradrenaline and you may remember that in Chapter 4 it was said to be bad for you. Well, that's what makes hormones so complicated. Noradrenaline released during periods of stress is bad for you. But when you're happy – when, for example, phenylethylamine is present – you'll feel great. And if dopamine is also present you'll feel euphoric. (You see, it's seldom a matter of any individual hormone acting alone, it's the cocktail.)

What's more, exercise isn't only exhilarating at the time. Regular exercise has an enduring effect that also helps keep you smiling through life's little crises.

Insight

If the word 'exercise' bothers you, call it something else. For example, you could call it, 'enjoying your body', or 'revelling in sensuality' or 'optimizing your physicality'. Birds swoop. Lambs gambol. Horses canter. Dolphins leap. Why? For the sheer pleasure of having a body and the thrill of moving it.

It isn't just a matter of producing happiness chemicals. And it isn't just a matter of strengthening your heart/lung system and various muscles. It's also about improving the function of just about every part of your organism. It's about feeling vital, animated, alive. It's about feeling and being healthy.

And when you feel healthy you tend to feel happy. In fact, in many studies, good health is rated second only to marriage as a fundamental cause of happiness; particularly for older people, who don't take it for granted the way younger people do. And it works both ways. Health equals happiness and happiness equals health.

But it doesn't stop there. People who exercise a little every week enjoy two extra years of life compared with the couch potatoes. And people who exercise a little more – but still only moderately – enjoy almost four extra years. Those who exercise regularly and vigorously gain as much as ten years, according to some researchers.

So what are you waiting for? Enjoying your body doesn't have to be painful, boring or repetitive. Think dancing. Think skiing. Think swimming. Think volleyball with friends on the beach. Think football. Whatever you fancy.

Keep smiling

My grandmother started walking five miles a day when she was 65. She's 76 now and we don't know where she is.

Even if you're convinced there's no form of exercise you'd like (you're wrong), remember this: just watching television will become more enjoyable as a result of exercising. In fact, everything you do will be enhanced because exercise not only gets the blood pumping into every corner of your body, but also every nook and cranny in your brain.

In Britain, about four-fifths of people don't get enough exercise. That's an awful lot of less-than-optimum happiness. Join the one-fifth who do! You'll:

▶ *feel happier*
▶ *sleep better*
▶ *have more energy*
▶ *look better*
▶ *enjoy greater self-esteem*
▶ *think more clearly (especially if you're older)*
▶ *handle stress more easily*
▶ *have a reduced risk of heart attack*
▶ *increase your levels of HDL or 'good' cholesterol*
▶ *lower your blood pressure*
▶ *increase your bone density*
▶ *boost your immune system*
▶ *enhance your sexual responsiveness*
▶ *increase your life expectancy.*

In other words, you'll be happy-fit.

The depression buster

Exercise is so good at improving mood that it's actually become a standard treatment for depression. In the UK, the National Institute for Health and Clinical Excellence (NICE) recommends exercise and psychotherapy, rather than antidepressants, as the first line of treatment for mild depression. In fact, it's beneficial for all types of depression. In carefully controlled trials, exercise has performed just as well as antidepressants in combating depression, but without the side effects of drugs.

Generating those happy chemicals

So why should exercise feel so good? When you think about it, it's not hard to understand how human beings evolved that way. Our ancestors had to be capable of vigorous activity if they were to eat. When their muscles screamed for respite, those whose bodies produced chemicals to ease the pain were the ones who ran down the prey and got the food. Logically, they were also the ones evolution selected. Well, that's a simplistic way of putting it, but right in essence. Nowadays we only have to be capable of lifting a can off a shelf, but our bodies remain unchanged. So if we want to enjoy those same chemicals, we have to exercise. Here are those happy chemicals:

▶ *Endorphins: the word means 'endogenous morphine', that's to say, morphine-like substances produced by the body. Endorphins combat pain, promote happiness and are one of the ingredients in the 'runner's high'.*

▶ *Phenylethylamine (PEA): this chemical is also found in chocolate as well as some fizzy drinks. Researchers at Rush University and the Center for Creative Development, Chicago, have demonstrated that PEA is a powerful antidepressant. Meanwhile, scientists at Nottingham Trent University in the UK have shown that PEA levels increase significantly following exercise.*

▶ *Noradrenaline/norepinephrine (NE): when generated by exercise, noradrenaline tends to make you feel happy, confident, positive and expansive.*

▶ *Serotonin: the link with exercise isn't so strong for this one, but serotonin is a neurotransmitter for happiness and there's reason to think exercise elevates its level in the brain.*

In addition, exercise lowers the level of:

▶ *cortisol: a stress hormone linked with low mood.*

There are also two further processes at work:

▶ *Thermogenics: exercise increases the body's core temperature, which in turn relaxes muscles, which in turn induces a feeling of tranquility.*

▶ *Right brain/left brain: repetitive physical activities such as jogging 'shut down' the left side of the brain (logical thought), freeing up the right brain (creative thought). It's a kind of meditation and it's why solutions to seemingly intractable problems often appear 'by magic' when exercising.*

How much exercise?

Remember that we're primarily looking at exercise as a source of happiness, not physical fitness. So how much exercise does it take to boost those all-important happiness chemicals? The good news is, surprisingly little. Let's take a look:

▸ *Endorphins: the level of beta-endorphins, the chemicals the body releases to combat pain, increases five times after 12 minutes of vigorous exercise.*
▸ *Phenylethylamine (PEA): the researchers at Nottingham Trent University found that running at 70 per cent of maximum heart rate (MHR – see below) for 30 minutes increased the level of phenylacetic acid in the urine (which reflects phenylethylamine) by 77 per cent.*
▸ *Noradrenaline/norepinephrine (NE): this increases up to ten times following eight minutes of vigorous exercise.*

Insight
It would seem that around ten minutes of vigorous exercise is already highly beneficial in terms of endorphins and NE, but that PEA levels are slower to augment.

HOW VIGOROUS IS VIGOROUS?

The word 'vigorous' may sound daunting, especially if you don't take any exercise at all at the moment. But, in reality, it doesn't take very long to achieve, even starting at zero.

You've probably got a pretty good idea already of what 'vigorous' feels like, but let's pin it down a little more scientifically.

Step 1: calculate your maximum heart rate
Your maximum heart rate (MHR) is the level at which your heart just can't beat any faster. It can be worked out in a fitness

laboratory, but there is an easier and less exhausting (although less precise) way to do it. To calculate your MHR use the following formula: 220 – your age. For example, if you're 40 years old your MHR will be: 220 – 40 = 180.

Step 2: calculate your training heart rate

Experts argue about the percentage of MHR that provides the best training heart rate (THR). But most people are agreed that as a minimum, THR should be at least 60 per cent of MHR. Beyond 70 per cent of MHR, exercise would be classed as 'vigorous'. At 70 to 80 per cent you'd be in the zone where aerobic conditioning improves the most. You wouldn't want to go beyond 80 per cent unless you were seriously training to win races. So let's stick with the assumption that you're 40 years old and intending to exercise at the 70 per cent level. The calculation would look like this:

$$(220 – 40) \times 70\% = 180 \times 70\% = 126.$$

At that level you should be able to carry on a conversation – with a little bit of puffing.

Step 3: discover your resting heart rate

Your resting heart rate (RHR) is the level when you wake up in the morning and before you get out of bed. It's the measure of how well your exercise programme is going. The average RHR for men is 60 to 80 beats per minute while for women it's somewhat higher at 70 to 90 beats a minute.

If you're at 100 beats or more you're clearly not getting sufficient exercise. You should be aiming to get below 60. Athletes tend to be in the range 40 to 50. RHRs under 30 have been known.

It's not possible to say that your RHR is directly linked to happiness, but there is an indirect link. If your RHR starts going down, it's a good indication that those happiness chemicals are being produced during exercise.

Problem: How will I know my heart rate?

The easiest place to take your pulse is to one side of your Adam's apple. Just press gently with three fingers and you'll feel it. Another place is on your wrist. Turn your hand palm upwards and place four fingers of your other hand lengthwise with your little finger at the base of your thumb. You should feel the pulse either under your forefinger or middle finger. Count for 15 seconds and multiply by four.

However, it's not very easy taking your pulse accurately while you're exercising. A better idea is to buy a heart rate monitor with a watch-style display on your wrist. They're available quite cheaply in sports equipment shops.

Keep smiling

The only reason I took up jogging was so I could hear heavy breathing again.

HOW LONG AND HOW OFTEN?

Asking how much exercise you need is a little bit like asking how many jokes you need or how much music you need. Come on, you've already forgotten that this is fun. However, since you ask, the minimum is 20 minutes of brisk exercise three times a week (and you'll need to allow five minutes at either end for warming up and cooling down).

Five times a week would be better. Longer sessions, within reason, would be better still. Dr James Blumenthal carried out a study on 150 depressed people, aged 50 or over, at Duke University in 1999. Not only did exercise substantially improve mood, but Dr Blumenthal concluded that for each 50-minute increment of exercise, there was an accompanying 50 per cent reduction in relapse rate. So even a little is good, but more is better (within reason).

> *The sooner you can take physical action when faced with stress, the less the stress will negatively affect you.*
>
> Dr Paul Rosch, Amercian specialist on stress

The runner's high

The so-called 'runner's high' is somewhat controversial. Some people say it exists and others say it doesn't. Those who say it does describe it as a state of euphoria, an altered state of consciousness or a physical style of meditation.

Of course, if it exists it wouldn't only be runners who experience it. It should equally come with any steady, repetitive exercise. In other words, you'd be far more likely to experience it in things like running, swimming, cycling and rowing than in stop-start sports such as tennis or basketball.

One marathon runner has written that: 'Anyone expecting a high or mystical experience during a run is headed for disappointment.' But many others insist that they do regularly enjoy such a state. The explanation probably lies at least partly in the nature of the exercise – neither too little nor, on the other hand, too gruelling.

It seems that those who push themselves very hard simply experience too much tedium, discomfort and pain to enjoy themselves. On the other hand, those who don't take things far enough never get to the point at which the runner's high starts to kick in.

But it's also a question of how you define words like 'high', 'euphoria', and 'mystical'. If you're expecting to come back from exercise a changed person, a sort of instant guru, then, of course, that isn't going to happen.

Here I'll declare myself on the side of the 'mystics'. For a bet at the age of 50 I agreed to run a marathon. I had just over nine months to prepare. A marathon is 26.2 miles (42.2 km) and at that point, I swear, I couldn't run more than 26 seconds without getting out of breath. I was starting from zero. Now it's a principle of amateur preparation that you never run a marathon in training. It's just too debilitating. So when you line up for your first ever marathon you don't know for sure that you can do it. In my case, the furthest I'd run was 20 miles. The extra six miles were unknown territory. Well, I did do it and for those last few miles I was flying. I'd followed a well-established training routine and it worked perfectly. I'm not exaggerating when I say I could have carried on running without any problem. Without doubt I was experiencing the runner's high and it lasted the rest of the day. (Next morning was a different story.)

Insight

What does the runner's high feel like? Different people describe it differently. I'd say a certain immunity from pain, both physical and mental, coupled with a sense of detachment and a quiet sort of happiness.

I've carried on running, although I've never attempted a marathon again, and nowadays I can get a runner's high at much shorter distances. The key ingredients seem to be these:

▶ *The exercise should be at around 70 per cent of MHR – high enough to generate those happy chemicals, low enough to avoid real discomfort or pain.*

- *Don't think about the exercise; instead, let your mind wander over pleasant subjects such as your relationship or the beauty of the countryside.*
- *Stick with one type of exercise; it seems to help if the body is familiar with it.*
- *Exercise regularly – say, five days a week.*
- *Don't expect to feel euphoria early on – it'll probably take a few months before you have your first experience.*
- *You'll usually need to exercise for around 30 minutes before you start to experience an altered state of consciousness.*
- *For the first 20 minutes, while your body cranks itself up, you'll more likely be wondering why you're doing it at all.*
- *At 30 minutes you may start to feel a mild euphoria.*
- *Between 45 minutes and an hour you may enter an altered state of consciousness.*

Insight

Once you've had the runner's high you'll find it comes more and more easily. You probably won't have the time or inclination to exercise for up to an hour regularly but you could aim to have, say, a one-hour session every weekend, coupled with two to four shorter sessions during the week. During that hour-long session you should get your runner's (or swimmer's or cyclist's or whatever's) high.

Keep smiling

I don't jog. It makes the ice jump right out of my glass.

Are you happy-fit?

Here are some simple tests for you to assess your fitness now. Try them again in a month, after you've got started on some exercise.

1 What's your resting heart rate (that is, your pulse when you wake up in the morning)?
   a   Under 50
   b   50–60
   c   60–70
   d   70–80
   e   80–90
   f   Over 90

2 Can you touch the floor with your legs straight? (Warm up a little before trying this.)
   a   I can touch the floor with the palms of my hands.
   b   I can touch the floor with the tips of my fingers.
   c   I can touch my ankle bones.
   d   I can't get further than my calves.

3 How many sit-ups can you do in one minute? (Don't do this if you have a back problem. To do sit-ups, lie on your back on the carpet, knees bent, heels about 45 cm (18 inches) from your buttocks, feet flat on the floor shoulder-width apart and anchored under a heavy piece of furniture. Your hands should be on the sides of your head. When reclining you only need to touch your shoulders to the floor.)
   a   More than 50
   b   40–50
   c   30–40
   d   20–30
   e   10–20

4 How long does it take you to walk half a mile? (Measure the distance along a flat stretch of road/pavement using your car.)
   a   Under 6 minnutes
   b   6–7 minutes
   c   7–8 minutes
   d   8–9 minutes
   e   9–10 minutes
   f   Over 10 minutes

Question 1

	Women	Men
a	25	23
b	20	18
c	15	13
d	10	8
e	5	3
f	0	0

Question 2

	Men			Women		
	Under 30	30–50	Over 50	Under 30	30–50	Over 50
a						
b	15	20	25	13	18	23
c	10	15	20	8	13	18
d	8	13	18	6	11	16
e	5	10	15	3	8	13

Question 3

	Men			Women		
	Under 30	30–50	Over 50	Under 30	30–50	Over 50
a	20	25	–	25	–	–
b	15	20	25	20	25	–
c	10	15	20	15	20	25
d	5	10	15	10	15	20
e	2	5	10	5	10	15

Question 4

| | Men | | | Women | | |
	Under 30	30–50	Over 50	Under 30	30–50	Over 50
a	20	25	–	25	–	–
b	15	20	25	20	25	–
c	10	15	20	15	20	25
d	5	10	15	10	15	20
e	1	5	10	5	10	15

What your score means

If you scored 75–100 you're already extremely fit and are no doubt already enjoying the happy bonus. If you scored 50–74 you're not in bad shape, but if you do a little more you'll gain benefits in terms of health as well as happiness. If you scored under 50 then, in one way, you're very lucky because you're going to improve rapidly once you start exercising regularly – you'll notice a difference in mood very quickly.

What type of exercise?

Below are some suggestions, but there are plenty of other things you can do – as long as you keep your heart beating at your THR for 20 minutes. The best exercise is something you enjoy and will be happy to do several times a week. It's no good relying on, say, a ski trip once a year or a game of tennis once a month. So when you're choosing, bear in mind practical considerations such as cost, distance from your home and the availability of friends (if it's something you can't do on your own).

Insight

If you're very resistant to the whole idea of exercise it's all the more important to find an activity that really inspires you. Something that has a point to it might do the trick. For example, rather than swim up and down in a pool, you might, over the course of the summer, swim along a whole

stretch of coastline, getting to know all the various bays.
A different kind of point can come from raising money for
charity through sponsored activities.

JOGGING

Jogging is a lot of fun. The steady, rhythmical movement seems
to generate more 'happy' chemicals per minute than many other
activities. Just think about it for a moment. Here's an exercise that:

▶ *doesn't require any special equipment*
▶ *doesn't have to cost anything*
▶ *doesn't require any special training*
▶ *provides plenty of fresh air and sunshine out of doors*
▶ *can be done indoors on a machine when the weather is bad*
▶ *can be done alone or with friends*
▶ *can be done anywhere*
▶ *enhances creative thinking and permits 'meditation'*
▶ *makes progress very easy to measure.*

For all those reasons, jogging is one of the very best things
you can do to get happy-fit. And even if you take up some
other activity, jogging is always a good thing to build into
your weekly routine.

Insight

One of the problems is running slowly enough. Yes, slowly.
Beginners tend to associate the word running with 'going
fast'. Wrong. Don't rush. You're aiming for a pace you can
sustain over a long period. That means going a lot slower
than your sprinting pace. In fact, to begin with you should
try to run no faster than the pace of a brisk walk. If you can
hardly speak you're going too fast.

Here's a little programme to help you build up from zero to a
reasonable level of happy-fitness in only ten weeks. At the end of it
you can just continue at the week-ten level on three to five days or,
if you really get inspired, you might like to run further.

Your ten-week jogging programme

Exercise for 20 minutes in accordance with the following programme, plus five minutes warming up and five minutes cooling down, making a total of 30 minutes in all. Exercise at least three times a week and build up to five times. Don't run too fast – at all times you should be able to carry on a conversation.

Week

1 Alternate 1 minute of running with 2 minutes of walking.
2 Alternate 2 minutes of running with 2 minutes of walking.
3 Alternate 3 minutes of running with 2 minutes of walking.
4 Alternate 5 minutes of running with 2 minutes of walking.
5 Alternate 6 minutes of running with 1.5 minutes of walking.
6 Alternate 8 minutes of running with 1.5 minutes of walking.
7 Run 10 minutes, walk 1.5 minutes, run 10 minutes.
8 Run 12 minutes, walk 1 minute, run 8 minutes.
9 Run 15 minutes, walk 1 minute, run 5 minutes.
10 Run 20 minutes.

Fun tips

▶ Wear something crazy.
▶ Wear a heart rate monitor.
▶ If you don't want to be alone, run with friends or a dog.

GYM

If you join a gym, you'll have access to all kinds of exercise equipment. There's almost certain to be a static bicycle, treadmill, rowing machine, weight-training machines, free weights, possibly a swimming pool and almost certainly classes in things like aerobic dance and yoga.

Membership of a gym:

▶ *doesn't require you to have any special equipment*
▶ *can be used whatever the weather*
▶ *can be visited alone or with friends*
▶ *can exercise a wide range of muscles as well as the heart/ lung system*

> ▶ *gives access to a professional on hand to advise and motivate you*
> ▶ *makes progress very easy to measure.*

But:

> ▶ *you will require training before you can use the equipment safely*
> ▶ *if the gym is a long way from home you may not always feel like going*
> ▶ *gyms are expensive.*

Fun tips
- ▶ Buy yourself some trendy exercise gear.
- ▶ Join some classes.
- ▶ Listen to your MP3 player if the gym doesn't have music TV.

DANCING

Now, dancing does sound like fun to a lot of people. But can something so, well, anti-puritan, actually make you healthier? It certainly can. Some people say the devil has all the best tunes but they're wrong (and we'll be seeing just how wrong in Chapter 10, which is all about happy-sex). Dancing has all the benefits of jogging plus a few more of its own. The only difference is that it's somewhat harder to measure progress.

Some styles of dancing incorporate meditation, such as 5Rhythms developed by Gabrielle Roth in the 1960s – a synthesis of indigenous dance, Eastern philosophy and modern psychology.

Fun tips
- ▶ Wear something crazy.
- ▶ Invite friends round for regular sessions.
- ▶ Try to find your own individual dance.

DON'T FORGET FLEXIBILITY

Being happy-fit includes being flexible, so don't forget to add some stretches into your exercise routine. On your days 'off' you could also try yoga, pilates or even juggling.

Keeping motivated

Knowing that exercise will make you happier as well as improving your health should be enough to make you throw down this book right now and head straight for the door. But, unfortunately, life isn't like that. We seldom do the things that are good for us and even if we start out with the best of intentions it's all too easy to backslide. So here are a few tips on keeping motivated:

▶ *Try to take your exercise regularly at a certain time every day, and on your days 'off' just go for a leisurely stroll; then, when the time comes round, your body will soon start demanding that you do something active with it.*

▶ *If your favourite exercise is out of doors, try to have an indoor back-up you can turn to in bad weather.*

▶ *Exercise together with friends and jolly each another along (unless, of course, you prefer to be alone).*

▶ *Don't strain; take it easy and build up gradually.*

▶ *Keep an exercise diary and enter your distances, times, heart rates, scores or whatever; look at it from time to time and take pride in your progress.*

▶ *Give yourself rewards whenever you achieve a particular goal; if it's a cup you covet, then award yourself a cup – or it could be new clothes, a meal out, a massage or whatever you fancy (and can afford).*

▶ *Hang up a poster of your ideal body; that's how you're going to look.*

▶ *Keep thinking of the health benefits – lower resting heart rate, blood pressure and weight, fewer health problems and 2–10 extra years of life.*

▶ *Maintain that 'happiness diary'. Does it show you're happier than you used to be? If you are, then for goodness sake don't stop.*

Keep smiling
If God had wanted us to touch our toes, He would have put them further up our bodies.

10 THINGS TO REMEMBER

1 *Exercise makes you happy because it releases various happy chemicals including endorphins, phenylethylamine and norepinephrine/noradrenaline; it also lowers cortisol, the stress hormone.*

2 *Exercise also improves just about every aspect of your life because it enhances the health of body and mind.*

3 *Exercise is recommended by the UK's National Institute for Health and Clinical Excellence (NICE) for the treatment of mild depression.*

4 *If you've been suffering from depression, the more you exercise the less you're likely to relapse.*

5 *The minimum amount of exercise for happy-fitness is 20 minutes three times a week.*

6 *You should exercise at around 70 per cent of your maximum heart rate (MHR).*

7 *When you exercise enough you can enter of a state of euphoria known as the 'runner's high' – but you can experience it in many activities.*

8 *Jogging is one of the most convenient ways to become happy-fit.*

9 *An exercise diary and rewards for reaching targets are ways of keeping motivated.*

10 *If you're not used to exercise, consult a doctor before starting an exercise programme.*

HOW HAPPY ARE YOU NOW?

Is exercise making you feel happier?

a *Yes.*
b *No – in fact it's making me feel depressed because it's too hard.*
c *No, I'm not doing any.*

If you answered '(a)' move on to the next chapter. If you answered '(b)' because it's been years since you took any vigorous exercise then it's bound to be difficult at first. Certainly don't feel depressed about it. In fact, the first few minutes of vigorous exercise are *always* a bit tough for everyone. It takes time for the body to 'get into gear', especially once you're over 40. And if, as a beginner, you're only exercising for a few minutes then, unfortunately, it's all pain because you never get to the pleasurable part. Check with your doctor to make sure there's no reason you shouldn't exercise. If you get the go ahead, then persevere a little longer. It will help enormously if you can find an activity that really inspires you. Read again the section on keeping motivated.

If you answered '(c)' and are not yet doing any exercise, read the whole chapter again. The science is there to back this up. Exercise is a powerful mood enhancer, at least as effective as antidepressants. So, if you really want to be happy, don't deny yourself this proven method.

Keep smiling

If you really, really can't find any form of exercise you enjoy, try the following:

▶ Start the ball rolling.
▶ Run round in circles.
▶ Jump to conclusions.
▶ Wade through the newspapers.
▶ Push your luck.
▶ Put your foot in your mouth.
▶ Hit the nail on the head.

8

Be happy being yourself

In this chapter you will learn:
- *how to achieve the maximum satisfaction of your whole being*
- *how you can run away to happiness*
- *why you should learn to say 'yes' more often*
- *why everything you do should express your personality.*

Life isn't about finding yourself. Life is about creating yourself.

George Bernard Shaw (1856–1950), Irish dramatist

The summit of happiness is reached when a person is ready to be what he is.

Erasmus (c.1466–1536), Dutch scholar

When asked what makes them happy, most people's immediate reaction is to mention very tangible things. Sometimes they're 'big' things like houses and cars; more often they're 'small' things like hearing their children laugh. But get down to the psychology of happiness and one issue comes up again and again. People are unhappy when they feel they're constrained and they're happy when they feel free to be themselves.

If you can't be yourself, you can't be happy. That's clear from what people say in surveys. You probably know it from your own life because very few of us are fortunate enough to be entirely 'happy in our own skins'. There's always something we're frightened of showing to the world. It can be for various reasons. It may be that we had overbearing, over-ambitious, controlling parents and are now too inhibited to reveal ourselves. It may be that the people who surround us are repressing us in some way.

George Bernard Shaw and Erasmus approach the question of who you are from different directions. The famous playwright was a man with little formal schooling who educated himself in the British Museum reading room. No wonder he saw himself as self-created. Erasmus, the sixteenth-century Dutch scholar with a long formal education, saw identity more as something inherent, which needs to be discovered.

As is so often the case, the truth lies in the middle. We're born with certain characteristics, as studies of identical twins separated at birth have shown very clearly. Our life experiences then build on that foundation. In practice, the precise balance between 'nature' and 'nurture' doesn't matter as much as that the blend of the two – the 'real you' – finds expression.

Maximum satisfaction

The shift comes about when we seriously ask ourselves: in what situation do I experience the maximum satisfaction of my whole being?

Arne Naess (1912–2009), Norwegian ecologist and philosopher

Making up your mind to be what you want and do what you want is only the beginning of the solution. Because you now have to find out what it is that you want. You might think you know. But you could very easily be mistaken.

Arne Naess was a Norwegian philosopher and 'deep ecologist'. He advised that each of us should ask ourselves: 'In what situation do I experience the maximum satisfaction of my whole being?' This is far more profound than it first seems. Think about it: the maximum satisfaction; your whole being. Suddenly, things like watching television and shopping go straight out the window. We're looking for things that are more fundamental and profound. More real.

Insight

So what are the things that give you the maximum satisfaction? What makes you feel physically, mentally and spiritually alive to the ultimate degree? Only *you* can answer that.

Try this

If you think you know the things that cause you to 'experience the maximum satisfaction' then, for this exercise, write down the number of hours a week you spend on those things. For example, your list might start like this:

Things that give 'maximum satisfaction'	Hours per week
Playing with my children	4
Making love with my partner	1
Hill walking	2

When you've done that, make a second list of all the other things, the things that don't give much satisfaction: the chores, the routines, the boring minutiae of existence. It might start like this:

Things that give 'minimum satisfaction'	Hours per week
Cooking and washing up	14
Commuting to work	15

Now compare the two lists. In all probability, you'll find you're spending at least six hours doing 'boring', minimal satisfaction things for every hour of 'maximum satisfaction'. It could even be that you've never yet experienced 'maximum satisfaction'.

Don't assume that life has to be that way. Just because thousands of other people commute long distances to work doesn't mean you have to. Just because thousands of other

(Contd)

people do jobs they don't enjoy doesn't mean you have to. Just because thousands of other people live somewhere boring doesn't mean you have to.

> **Insight**
>
> If the list you've just compiled is going to be more than an entertaining experiment, you've got to make up your mind to take control of your life. You've got to be absolutely determined to increase the amount of time you spend on the 'maximum' things and reduce the amount of time you spend on the 'minimum' things.

ACHIEVING THE MAXIMUM

But the problem is that we don't always know what gives us the 'maximum satisfaction'. We tend to equate it with fulfilling our major ambitions and fantasies, and they are usually handed down to us by other people: 'I'd get the maximum satisfaction from driving around in a sports car.' 'I'd get the maximum satisfaction from being a celebrity.' But if we ever achieved these fantasies, in all probability we would soon find the excitement palls.

So how can we find the source of 'maximum satisfaction'? Easy to ask. Very hard to do. When you have people expecting you to behave in a particular way, when you have people pressuring you to conform, how can you become the real you?

Running away to happiness

One Law for the Lion & Ox is Oppression.

William Blake (1757–1827), English poet and mystic

From the time we're very young we're usually told we mustn't run away from things. It's also the message of countless books and films. The hero is a man or woman who stands up against all odds. Well, that's fine in fiction. But real life is different. If you want to be happy, you have to learn not only that you can run away but that sometimes you must run away. Otherwise you're stuck with situations in which you arrived through somebody else's choice, through your own ignorance or simply by accident. So run away and be proud of it, because it's the rational thing to do.

When you're young and inexperienced you can't know what makes you happy. You can't know if you're a lion or an ox. That's something you can only find out from trial and error. If you don't learn to run away then you're going to be stuck with the very first thing you try. You're going to be lumbered with the first girl or boy you ever go out with, the first employer who ever takes you on and the first town you ever decide to live in.

What's more – and this is very important – you can't even know what things you might like to try. It's quite possible that the very thing that could make you happy is something you haven't even heard of yet. But while you're running you'll encounter all kinds of new situations and, one day, you'll find, perhaps purely by chance, the one that really makes you happy.

Let's try to define what's meant by 'running away' here. It doesn't mean leaving home at age 15 without telling anybody. It doesn't mean dumping your wife and children without support. It doesn't mean leaving work without giving notice. But it is the very opposite of that old-fashioned advice: 'You've made your bed and now you've got to lie in it.' You haven't got to lie in it. In fact, if you're not happy, it will be better for everybody if you find another 'bed'. Here's why:

▶ *If you're not very good at your job (because it's not what you really want to do) then it's not just you that's suffering. It's also the company and your fellow employees. If you change to a job you do like, everyone will benefit.*

- *If you're not actually in love with your partner then it's not just you that's suffering. He/she's suffering as well. A separation/divorce will give you both the chance to find true love.*
- *If you're not happy with your university course then it's not just you that's suffering. It's your tutor, the university and the taxpayer as well. Changing to the right course is in everyone's interests.*

Of course, some people are happy with the cards that fate has dealt them. You're almost bound to feel comfortable in the place you were brought up. The landscape, the buildings, the climate, the way people dress and talk and behave will all be familiar. Somehow they'll probably seem 'right' precisely because you're used to them. That's why so many people insist: 'My country is the best country in the world.'

But not every country can be the 'best country in the world'. Isn't it more sensible to try a few before deciding? And for 'country' you can also substitute town, job, hobby and plenty of other things.

Twenty years from now you will be more disappointed by the things you didn't do than by the ones you did do. So throw off the bowlines. Sail away from the safe harbour. Catch the trade winds in your sails. Explore. Dream. Discover.

Mark Twain (1835–1910), American writer

Try this
While you're 'running away', don't run so fast that you haven't got time to enjoy everything you pass. The more things you take an interest in, the more possibilities you have for being happy.

So for today, show an interest in everything. When you see a flower, stop and count the petals and take careful note of the colour of the stamens (the male bits that produce the pollen). When you pass a tree, stop and take careful note of the bark; touch it with your hand. Whenever you meet anyone, find out something about them. When you're confronted with a piece of equipment, find out how it works.

Running away to the sunshine

Quite a lot of people in northern latitudes dream
of running away to the sunshine. Perhaps you're one of
them. It makes good sense if you're one of those people
who feels low in winter. Quite simply, some bodies just
don't work very well when there's too little daylight. Lack
of light causes a reduction in serotonin (a neurotransmitter
that makes us feel happy) and an increase in melatonin
(which makes us sleepy). It's a condition known as seasonal
affective disorder (SAD).

There are three possible solutions:

1 Learn to be happy despite the lack of sunlight.
2 Enjoy 'artificial sunlight' every day in winter.
3 Move somewhere with more sunshine in winter.

Don't forget that if you're British, or, indeed, a citizen of any
member of the European Union, you have the right to live
and work in most other member states. A few members are
not yet up to speed but, if it's sunshine you want and need,
then nobody can stop you going to find it in Portugal,
Spain (including the Canary Islands, which are only just
outside the tropics), the south of France, Italy or Greece, to
name a few places. Don't think only in terms of the coast.
You'll also find bags of sunshine in winter at altitude in the
Pyrenees and the Alps – at 1,000 metres or more you'll often
be above the clouds while everyone else suffers. Of course,
it won't be hot up a mountain in winter but that doesn't
matter where SAD is concerned.

If you're an American citizen you similarly have the right to
live almost as far south as the Tropic of Cancer.

Millions of people have already done it. Why not you?

(Contd)

But if you can't move for whatever reason, you can get some of the benefits of sunlight artificially by using special SAD light boxes. Here's an idea of the light intensities:

▶ *typical home or office lighting – 200–500 lux*
▶ *cheap SAD light box – 2,500 lux*
▶ *top-end SAD light box – 10,000 lux*
▶ *bright summer day – 100,000 lux.*

Obviously, a light box that emits 10,000 lux will be effective in a much shorter time than one that only emits 2,500 lux (say, 30 minutes per session as opposed to two hours). So it makes sense to get the best you can afford. Having said that, you can get on with other things while you're receiving the light therapy. Just sit close to it while you're having a meal, reading or doing some office jobs, for example. (In fact, you shouldn't look directly at the light.) So, if you have the opportunity to be by your light box for two hours every day the highest power may not be vital in your case.

Doing what you want

> *If there is a path it is someone else's path and you are not on the adventure.*
>
> Joseph Campbell (1904–87), American writer

In our lives we are often advised to follow the path less travelled. But, in fact, Joseph Campbell was absolutely right. Even that's not good enough. Whenever you follow an existing path you're not being yourself. You should aim to make your own path. If that happens to be very similar to many other paths that's fine. But if, like the Starship Enterprise, you want to go where no man or woman has ever been before then don't be put off. You don't have to be afraid of being different. The important point is that it's the path *you* want. Not a path someone else has told you to follow.

Sooner murder an infant in its cradle than nurse unacted desires.

Ask yourself how many times things you've done have made you unhappy. Now ask yourself how many times you've been unhappy because you didn't do something you wanted to do. In all probability you will think of ten times more of the latter than the former. The fact is it's what we don't do that usually makes us most unhappy.

It's the person we didn't ask out, the time we didn't say 'I love you', the exam we didn't study for, the travel opportunity we didn't take, the job we didn't apply for, and so on.

This is the meaning of Blake's proverb. He's not actually suggesting anyone should murder a baby. In fact, the baby in the proverb is you. Blake is saying that if you don't do the things you want to do in life then it's as if you'd been murdered as a baby. You're not fulfilling your promise. You're not becoming what you could have become. The person you should have been is effectively dead. Murdered.

Insight

Remember that Blake was writing about 'unacted *desires*'. You don't have to do something you *don't* want because you're afraid other people will think you're too conventional. It's fine to be conventional – just as long as you're sure that you are.

Learning to say 'yes'

But if a man doesn't break the string, tell me, what flavour is left in life? You're young, you have money, health, you're a good fellow, you lack nothing. Nothing, by thunder! Except just one thing – folly!

Nikos Kazantzakis (1885–1957), Greek writer, in his novel Zorba The Greek

It's very easy to say 'no'. And sometimes, of course, very necessary and sensible. When you say 'no' you can usually predict the outcome with certainty. 'No' means that everything stays as it is. So 'no' is the safe option.

But sometimes it's far more interesting to take the unsafe option and say 'yes'. When you say 'yes' you embark on a journey whose outcome is unknown.

Of course, we have to get this business of 'no' and 'yes' into perspective. There are many things to which we must say 'no'. But some people say 'no' to almost anything that's new. They say 'no' to whatever threatens to disturb their routine and their security, 'no' to new ideas, 'no' to new situations. If you were utterly positive that the status quo is exactly what you want, you probably wouldn't be reading this book now. The fact is that lots of people say 'no' but regret it afterwards.

Keep smiling
I don't suffer from insanity, I enjoy every minute of it.

Try this
If the following suggestions were made to you, what would you answer? Yes or no?

- ▶ *Let's go on holiday to a country we've never visited before.*
- ▶ *Let's sell up and move to a new country.*
- ▶ *Let's live on a boat.*
- ▶ *Let's get backpacks/a motorbike and travel round the world.*
- ▶ *Let's build our own house, exactly as we want it.*
- ▶ *Let's make love in a position we've never tried before.*
- ▶ *Let's find jobs/work doing the things we really want to do.*
- ▶ *Let's give up our jobs and start our own business.*
- ▶ *Let's have makeovers and completely change the way we look.*
- ▶ *Let's take up an adrenaline sport.*
- ▶ *Let's go to evening classes to learn a new skill.*
- ▶ *Let's adopt orphans/take in refugees.*

There are 12 suggestions here. How many would you be willing to consider? Before you answer, let's take a look at the true story of Richard.

Following his divorce, a horse trainer called Richard bought some land in the middle of nowhere on which he intended to live in a mobile home and lick his wounds, far from everyone. That was the plan. Today, he heads a charitable foundation that, in the peace and quiet of the countryside, helps people who've been traumatized. This dramatic change came about because Richard said 'yes'. He said 'yes' to a woman he met by chance who told him his land was far too beautiful for him to keep all for himself. She suggested that he 'shared' it. And that's what he did. Using horses, he helps diagnose and treat people who are troubled and depressed – a fascinating new approach known as equitherapy.

Today Richard is a happy man – a very happy man. He could easily have said 'no'. Most people would have done. But he was curious to know what would happen if he said 'yes'.

Security is mostly a superstition. It does not exist in nature, nor do children of men as a whole experience it. Avoiding danger is no safer in the long run than outright exposure. Life is either a daring adventure, or nothing.

Helen Keller (1880–1968), American campaigner for the blind

So back to those questions. To how many would you answer 'yes'? Ten? Then you're obviously very adventurous and optimistic. And a bit wild. You take risks and things sometimes go wrong but you probably don't mind. Five? You're certainly open to new ideas but you like to weigh them up before you act. Two? One? None? Then you need to ask yourself, are you simply very fortunate and contented or are you, perhaps, afraid of life?

(Contd)

These are big things. But, so often, happiness comes from seemingly little things. It could come when you're hosing the flowers and you get the urge to spray your partner instead. It could come at a dinner party when you get the urge to make a controversial remark or tell a particularly risqué joke. It could come when you're on a deserted beach and you get the urge to throw off your clothes and swim naked. It could come at a social gathering when you get the urge to put your arms round the two nearest guests and sing a song.

Insight

The seemingly 'little things' are often the ones to do with the most profound issues of the human spirit. They're to do with inhibition and liberation. They're to do with being yourself, with self-expression, with being comfortable in your own skin. Find time for them.

There's a lovely scene in the 1989 film *Shirley Valentine* in which, while decorating a room, Pauline Collins and Bernard Hill end up happily slapping gunk over one another. It's a tiny moment in their relationship when they're suddenly free – perhaps it was the only one in their entire lives together.

Of course, there are many laws, rules, conventions and manners we have to observe if we're going to live alongside other people. Even, indeed, to live on our own. But some are imposed solely for the benefit of others. Some are based on old-fashioned ignorance and take no account of modern knowledge. Yet another category applies only to special situations, such as childhood, but nevertheless carries on into our adult lives.

What would happen if we actually did some of these things? Curiously, most of us admire the rare few who do. And yet we don't dare to be like it ourselves.

Are you sure? How important are all those other things you've just got to do? Does it matter if the car isn't shiny? Wouldn't letting the grass grow be good for insects and birds? Do the kids really want you to take them to all those after-school activities? Are you certain it's essential to have dinner with those people you don't really like?

Always ask yourself, 'To what extent will this give me the maximum satisfaction of my whole being?'

You'll probably find you have more time than you think.

Let go your inner child

We're often told to get in touch with our 'inner child'. We all know what it means. It's the idea that our 'inner child' is playful and carefree and that by being childlike once more we can be happy as adults.

However, the reality of childhood is somewhat different. Childhood isn't a free time. On the contrary, it's a straightjacket, or rather the struggle to put you into a straightjacket. As a child you were told you can't do this, you can't do that, you can't do the other. And there are usually perfectly good reasons. As a child you lack the necessary qualities (knowledge, judgement, wisdom, strength and so forth) to deal with certain situations. The problem is that we carry these admonitions on into adulthood. No one ever says to us: 'As from today that rule no longer applies.' It's just taken for granted that we'll 'grow up'. But we don't. At least, not completely. At the back of our minds we still harbour those ideas.

We still hear the voices of our childhood friends cautioning: 'You're not allowed to do that.'

So get in touch with your inner child. And when you have... Let it go. Become an adult. Cut yourself free.

Keep smiling

Psychoanalysis is much quicker for men than for women. When analysts want to take patients back to childhood, men are already there.

Expressing the real you

You'll almost certainly feel much happier if you express your unique personality in every way you can. That means being creative. Put your personal stamp on everything. Let's start with one of the most obvious ways.

CLOTHES AND HAIR

Take a look at your clothes. Take a look at your hair.

Don't ask yourself:

▶ *Do I look pretty/handsome?*
▶ *Do I look cool?*
▶ *Do I look smart?*
▶ *Do I fit in with everybody else?*

Instead, ask yourself this:

▶ *Do I look like me?*

Do you, in fact, even know what you look like? If your essence, your soul if you like, could walk and talk and dress, would it look the way you look now? Or would it be something different? Would it have longer hair? Shorter hair? A moustache? Bolder colours? A longer skirt? A shorter skirt? A younger style? A more classic style? What?

Of course, it may well be the case that a conventional appearance does represent the real you. That's fine. But if you feel differently don't be afraid to show it.

You can't be happy if you think, for whatever reason, that you have to keep the real you hidden away. Your clothes and your hairstyle are only the beginning.

Darren's story

I like to go horse riding and before I leave the house I put on the theme tune from *The Magnificent Seven*. Some people think I'm a little crazy. I even have a cowboy saddle, hat, chaps and spurs. But where's the harm? On the contrary, I love the relaxed style of Western riding and I enjoy myself more. The music transports me very quickly. It helps me get 'psyched up', especially if I know I might be going to face a challenging horse.

WORK

What work do you do?

- ▶ *The same kind of work as my father/mother/grandfather/ grandmother.*
- ▶ *The same kind of work as everyone else where I live.*
- ▶ *Something completely original.*

Most of us will spend something like a third of our waking hours as adults travelling to work and working. So if you're not happy with your job, you're not going to be very happy with your life. According to one researcher, marital happiness was the greatest source of overall happiness, but job dissatisfaction was the greatest source of unhappiness. In fact, you're at an increased risk of depression if you find your work undemanding and boring, but at an even greater risk if you find it too demanding. Depression tends to be lowest when the demands of the job are just right, neither too low nor too high.

In general, people want to work. Work gives life meaning and, for men, it fulfils the role that used to be the function of hunting. A study in the USA concluded that for every percentage increase in unemployment, murders went up 5.7 per cent, suicides 4.1 per cent and prison admissions 4 per cent. In another survey, two-thirds of people said they would want to continue working even if it wasn't financially necessary, although only one-third would continue with their present jobs. Not surprisingly, job satisfaction is highest among ABC1s, but only half as high among C2DEs.

What is it that creates the sense of satisfaction? One researcher found five key elements. A satisfying job:

▶ *allows a measure of independence and discretion in making decisions*
▶ *calls for a variety of skills*
▶ *provides feedback on how successfully the job has been done*
▶ *helps other people*
▶ *involves distinct tasks which can be completed.*

In addition, there are all the other things associated with work including, of course, money as well as friendship with colleagues.

Since stress leads to unhappiness it isn't a good idea, however, to have a stressful job. On a scale of zero to ten, being a miner was rated the most stressful job in Britain (8.3), followed by being in the police, a construction worker, a journalist, a pilot, and a prison officer. Being a manager was rated 5.8 and a diplomat 4.8. The most stressful jobs are clearly not the best paid.

The message from the research is clear. Get a job that:

▶ *gives plenty of satisfaction*
▶ *stretches you but is within your capabilities.*

On top of that, make sure your job reflects your real self.

The person who is a master in the art of living makes little distinction between their work and their play, their labour and their leisure, their mind and their body, their education and their recreation, their love and their religion.

They hardly know which is which. They simply pursue their vision of excellence and grace in whatever they do, leaving others to decide whether they are working or playing. To them, they are always doing both.

Zen Buddhist text

YOUR HOME

Where do you live?

▶ *Within 10 miles (16 km) of where I grew up.*
▶ *Between 10 and 50 miles (16–80 km) from where I grew up.*
▶ *Between 50 and 250 miles (80–400 km) from where I grew up.*
▶ *In a different country from where I grew up.*

Where you live could be vitally important to your external happiness. Because where you live dictates so much of what you do, who you know and even what illnesses you get. If you live close to where you grew up then, of course, it may be the place you'll be happiest. But remember that where you grew up was purely a matter of chance as far as you're concerned. Where you live should be a conscious decision and a reflection of the real you. Take a look again at the section earlier on running away.

And what about your home itself? What does it say about you? Does it reflect your personality? If not, get busy and make it into a statement. If you want to paint the walls black, paint them black.

We were watching a film together and it had a pretty sexy scene in it. You couldn't see exactly what was going on but it was something that we'd never done together, although I'd always wanted to. And I looked at my partner and said: 'We could do that.' And he said: 'OK, let's try.' And it was great. But it was also kind of sad that I'd never dared to suggest it before.

Try this
**You can express yourself in all kinds of other ways:
photography, painting, sculpting, writing, flower arranging,
gardening, cooking and much more.** In fact, everything you
do should be a statement about you.

1 *Ask your partner and people close to you if they can answer
the following questions about you:*

   ▷ *Who did I vote for in the last election?*
   ▷ *Can you name one of my favourite books/pieces of
   music/paintings/websites?*
   ▷ *What job would I choose if I could do anything
   I wanted?*
   ▷ *If money were no object, where would I go on holiday?*
   ▷ *Can you name the thing I'd most like to do in my life?*
   ▷ *What do you think I'd most like to change in my life?*
   ▷ *Would you say I am happy?*
   ▷ *Do you know my opinion on:*
      – *euthanasia?*
      – *the legalization of recreational drugs?*
      – *gay marriage?*
      – *the chance of life on another planet?*
      – *the possibility of life after death?*
      – *the existence of God?*
      – *the probability of climate change?*
      – *the growth of world population?*
      – *contraception?*

- *abortion?*
- *vegetarianism?*
- *feminism?*
- *the state of democracy?*

Score

20+ correct: you're not hiding anything much and that's very good for your happiness.

15–19 correct: you obviously let people around you know your opinion on most things but you could still go a little further.

10–14: you're not exactly secretive but you're far from comfortable with yourself – you'll feel a lot happier if you can open up a bit more.

9 or under: you're keeping yourself hidden away from other people and that's having a negative effect on your happiness – try harder to overcome your inhibitions and reveal yourself to others.

2 *Make a list of ten realistic things you'd like to do but have never dared. Then do them. If any involve or affect other people, discuss them with the person or persons concerned. If they don't agree then, of course, you have to accept that. But it could be that they're suffering from the same inhibitions you are. Give them the chance to break free as well. And while you're at it, suggest that they, too, make a list of the ten things they'd most like to do.*

Problem: I'm too inhibited to do what I want

If you're inhibited by your perception of what other people consider acceptable, bear in mind that other people are inhibited, too. If you take your lead from them you're never going to break free and be yourself. Don't be afraid to break new ground. Indeed, it may well be that if you take the lead, they'll follow you.

Just take it very slowly, one step at a time. It's important to move ahead but, on the other hand, there's no rush. You have a lifetime to deal with your inhibitions and that's often what it takes. But it's great fun.

Our own life is the instrument with which we experiment with the truth.

Thich Nhat Hanh (1926–), Buddhist teacher

Insight

What happens if the 'real you' turns out to be a rather miserable person? In fact, that's impossible. But it may be that you erroneously *see* yourself in that sort of light. Here's a way of changing that self-image. Think of someone you know or have seen on television who is extremely happy. Someone who optimistically deals with life's challenges and gaily transforms problems into opportunities. Someone who laughs a lot. Next, put that person into a scene from your own life. See them dealing with your situation easily, confidently and happily. Try to understand *how* they can be so cheerful. Finally, imagine yourself changing places with that person in this 'film' you're watching in your mind. See yourself handling life in exactly the same capable, optimistic and humorous manner.

Avoiding unhappiness

The flip side of doing what makes you happy is, of course, avoiding things that make you unhappy. A lot of Eastern philosophy tends to start with the proposition that that's more or less impossible. That life is full of unavoidable suffering. That the only possible course is to be mentally prepared for it.

But is that really true? Actually, it's not. In the West today life is very different from, say, the India of 2,500 years ago in the time of the Buddha when death was an everyday thing. Life then for many people was little other than suffering. But it isn't the case for the majority of people in the West now.

Many of the problems people do suffer in the West are avoidable as a lot of suffering is self-inflicted.

In Chapter 3 we saw the impact of negative thinking. In Chapter 4 we saw the impact of negative emotions. There are also negative actions. You're inviting a negative outcome if, for example, you smoke, eat unhealthily, drink too much alcohol or fail to have sufficient exercise.

So many problems we have in our lives are actually brought on by ourselves. Before you do something, ask:

▶ *Is this likely to make me happy at any time?*
▶ *Is this likely to make me unhappy at some other time?*

Insight

We're all motivated *towards* nice things and *away* from unpleasant things. But, in any given situation, some of us are moved far more by one type of motivation than the other. Try to work out which kind of motivation works best for you. For example, if you're trying to give up smoking, is it because you want to move *away* from ill health and expense or is it because you want to move *towards* more sporting prowess and whiter teeth? Understanding the direction of your motivation can help you be more effective when making changes in your lifestyle.

Plan your happy future

Put your stamp on the future as well as on the present. Don't leave others to take care of it or leave it to take care of itself. Ask yourself:

- ▶ *What would I like to be doing in three months' time?*
- ▶ *What would I like to be doing in a year's time?*
- ▶ *What would I like to be doing in five years' time?*

Work out a strategy. Set the wheels in motion. It's important for happiness that you always have, at the very least, one project underway and that you look forward to it.

> **When you stand in that sliver of space that is completely and utterly you, then will you be truly awesome, wonderful, magnificent.**
>
> Joseph Riggio, lifestyle guru

10 THINGS TO REMEMBER

1 Some of who you are was inborn, but that still leaves plenty of scope for you to create yourself – if you can't be yourself you can't be happy

2 Aim as much as possible for the maximum satisfaction of your whole being.

3 Don't be afraid to run away; it's futile to stay in a situation that is unhappy for everybody – and while you're running you'll discover new things.

4 Running away to the sunshine is the best solution to seasonal affective disorder (SAD).

5 Don't follow the well-trodden path or even the less-travelled path but make your own path.

6 Try saying 'yes' more often.

7 Let go of your inner child and let a fun-loving adult escape.

8 Be creative – express yourself in everything you do, from the way you dress to the way you decorate your home.

9 Job dissatisfaction is a major cause of unhappiness – find a job in which you can express your personality.

10 Devise projects for the future and look forward to them.

HOW HAPPY ARE YOU NOW?

Have you discovered what gives you 'the maximum satisfaction of your whole being'?

   a   *Yes, and it's great.*
   b   *Yes, but it just isn't practical for me to live*
       that way.
   c   *No.*

If you answered '(a)' to this (and the other two questions on this page) you're ready to move on to the next chapter. If you answered '(b)', read this chapter again and also review the material on negative thoughts and emotions in Chapters 2–4. If you answered '(c)' because you haven't yet discovered what causes 'the maximum satisfaction of your whole being', that's perfectly normal. People are very bad at predicting what will make them happy and a lot of such discovery comes about by accident. Read again the section on *Running away to happiness* – and start running.

Has being more 'you' made you any happier?

   a   *Yes.*
   b   *No – I've made changes but I feel just the same.*
   c   *I haven't made any changes.*

If you answered '(a)' to this (and the other two questions on this page) you're ready to move on to the next chapter. If you answered '(b)', are you sure you're being honest with yourself? It's almost impossible that greater self-expression wouldn't result in feeling happier. Almost certainly you haven't yet given voice to the 'real you'. Read this chapter again. If you answered '(c)' and haven't actually made any changes at all, then you also need to reread the chapter. It's rare to reach a state in which no further expansion of self-expression is possible. Take a good look at your life to see where more could be done.

Have you been able to avoid some sources of potential unhappiness?

a *Yes.*
b *No – I'm aware of them but I can't change.*

If you answered '(a)' to this (and the other two questions on this page) you're ready to move on to the next chapter. If you answered '(b)' then, of course, making certain kinds of changes, such as giving up smoking or cutting down on alcohol, can be difficult. And it's true, indeed, that a great deal of happiness can come from high-risk activities. Is there really any difference between smoking and, say, mountain climbing? Only you can answer that. Many people are willing to risk their health, their lives and possibly their future happiness in, for example, extreme sports. The happiness they get right now outweighs the other considerations. The important thing is to know the risks and to make your own properly informed decision. But there are other kinds of things that don't involve the same kind of balancing act. Do you always put on your seat belt? Do you wear a helmet when horse riding? Do you tell someone where you're going and what time you expect to be back when you set off on a wilderness hike? These are the kinds of things that have plenty of upside and no downside.

> *Don't ask yourself what the world needs; ask yourself what makes you come alive. And then go and do that. Because what the world needs is people who have come alive.*
>
> Dr Howard Thurman (1900–81), American author and civil rights leader

Keep smiling

'Doctor, I keep thinking I'm a wheelbarrow.'

'Yes, well, you must stop letting people push you around.'

9

Relationships, love and happiness

In this chapter you will learn:
- *what our pets can teach us about relationships*
- *why relationships are the number one source of happiness*
- *why 'projecting' will always end badly*
- *why 'acceptance' is the key to happy relationships.*

> *Of all the means which wisdom acquires to ensure happiness throughout the whole life, by far the most important is friendship.*
>
> Epicurus (341–270 BCE), Greek philosopher

> *God heard us. He sent help. He sent you.*
>
> Marianne Williamson (1952–), American spiritual activist

To be really lonely is an awful thing. In the nineteenth century, the pioneering French sociologist Emile Durkheim showed it could even be a death sentence. He discovered that the rate of suicide was higher among the unmarried and divorced than among the married, higher in childless marriages than those with children, higher in urban areas than in villages, higher among loners than among those with plenty of friends.

For social animals, separation means danger. Security comes from being with the family or group. Bad behaviour is punished by being driven out to the periphery of the herd, there to be the most likely target for any predators in the area. Understandably, animals are very anxious to be accepted back within the group as soon as possible. Never forget that you, too, are a social animal.

If you want to predict whether or not people are likely to be happy, you need do little more than assess the quality of their relationships. We depend on relationships as surely as we depend on air. In survey after survey, the conclusion is the same. Relationships are the single most important source of human happiness. On average:

- *People who are married or living with someone are happier than people who live alone.*
- *People who are close to their relatives are happier than people who aren't.*
- *People who have close friends are happier than people who don't.*
- *People who get on well with colleagues are happier than people who experience friction at work.*
- *People who have pets are less stressed, more long-lived and happier than those who don't.*

Keep smiling

A lonely person goes to see a psychotherapist.

'I have trouble making friends and I'm wondering if you can help – useless as people like you generally are.'

Pets

I'm going to start with pets because it's with our pets we have the least complicated relationships, and, in a way, the best. You might think I'm being facetious but I'm not. Just think about it for a moment – the way we love our pets, and the way they love us, is a model for what human relationships should be.

Your love for Fido doesn't depend on him being the most beautiful dog, nor the most intelligent, nor the most useful, nor anything like that. And Fido's love for you doesn't depend on your looks either, nor your wealth, nor the size of your house, nor anything of that kind. Basically, you love Fido because he loves you. And he loves you because you love him. It's unconditional love.

Stories of the devotion of animals are legion. A terrier that remained for weeks by the body of its dead master in the Lake District in 1805 was commemorated in a painting by Landseer and in a poem by Wordsworth who recorded:

> *Yes, proof was plain that, since the day*
> *When this ill-fated Traveller died,*
> *The Dog had watched about the spot,*
> *Or by his master's side...*

Fido's unconditional love does a lot more for you than you may have realized. Hanging out with Fido and, in particular, stroking him:

- *lowers your blood pressure*
- *reduces your level of the stress hormone cortisol*
- *increases your level of oxytocin – a peptide that makes you feel affectionate as well as, in turn, increasing the 'happy chemicals' dopamine and serotonin.*

Insight

In one study, the survival rate for heart-attack patients was 28 per cent higher if there was a pet in the house. The effects are so clear that many hospitals and hospices have animals that visit the patients.

The curious thing is that all of the positive effects can also be achieved through loving physical contact with other people. The fact that animals make such a clear difference is proof that we seldom get our human relationships right.

It's all down to expecting too much of the wrong kinds of things from our friends, relatives and partners. And we end up getting less of what we really need. Enjoy people as you enjoy your pet. Don't complicate things. Enjoy them for what they are. And not for what they can do for you.

Pets have other things to teach us, too, such as 'seeing' emotions – which is why your dog disappears the morning before an appointment at the vet or why your horse refuses to be caught when you need to give an injection. When you interact with animals you have to learn to get rid of your negative emotions – genuinely get rid of them – because animals can read you like a book. That's how they survive.

Insight

A pet, particularly a dog or a horse, is also a doorway back into the Nature from which so many of us are now unhappily estranged. I'll have more to say about this in Chapter 11.

Of course, merely buying a pet (or, better still, adopting one from a rescue centre) isn't immediately going to make a profound contribution to your baseline happiness. But as time goes by, and you bond, so you'll feel the benefits. But don't forget that animals also have rights and needs. Only get a pet if you're sure you can look after it properly for its whole life.

Here's a little joke about the difference between relationships with other humans and dogs – but, like all good jokes, it has a certain truth about it.

Keep smiling

A dog can be better than a new relationship because:

▶ *A dog never wants to know about every other dog you've had.*
▶ *After a year a dog is still pleased to see you.*
▶ *The later you are, the more pleased the dog is.*
▶ *A dog never needs to examine the relationship.*
▶ *A dog never criticizes.*

Insight

Not every dog or cat turns out to be your best friend. There can be personality clashes and some breeds are more difficult to handle than others. Take advice from people who have pets already, and don't rush in. Take time over your choice. Where dogs are concerned, professional help with training can be a good idea.

Human relationships

To eat and drink without a friend is to devour like the lion and the wolf.

Epicurus (341–270 bce), Greek philosopher

BE TACTILE

We're going to apply the first lesson you've learned from your pet. Count the number of times you stroke your pet in a day. Now resolve that you'll have at least the same amount of physical contact with everyone who's close to you.

You see, we often forget that we, too, are animals and need to touch and be touched. Why should we have less of this wonderful tonic than a dog does? We cover our bodies completely with clothes most of the time, which already makes it difficult, and, on top of that, we've introduced dangerous social conventions. That we've now become afraid to touch one another is a disaster for happiness.

The amazing substance oxytocin, which increases in your body when you stroke your pet, is vital to your mental health and happiness. But it's no use relying on your dog or cat as your sole source as oxytocin binds you to whatever you're touching.

In other words, if you want to feel bonded with someone and you want that person to feel bonded with you, touch. Of course, if someone doesn't want to be touched by you they're not going to like you because you touch them. Probably the reverse is true. I'm talking about your partner, your children, your brothers and sisters, your friends and so on – people who do want to be close to you.

Oxytocin's extraordinary role began when you were born. It was responsible for your mother's contractions, it was responsible for making milk flow from her breasts, it was responsible for making her maternal and your father paternal, it made your parents more likely to stick together and it was why they didn't abandon you when you cried for the hundredth time in a day. On top of all that, it helped your brain develop properly – without it some of your brain cells would have died. So if it hadn't been for touch and oxytocin your life would have been so very different.

Try this
Get touching and hugging at once. Here's what to do right now:

▶ *If you have a partner give him or her a hug. Find some place you can put your hand on bare skin.*

(Contd)

> ▶ *If you have children give them a hug. If they refuse to be hugged then, at least, deliver a slap on the back or a squeeze of the shoulders – the very minimum is a high five.*
>
> ▶ *If you have parents, sisters, brothers, whatever, give them all a hug.*
>
> ▶ *If you have a dog or a cat or any cuddly pet go and stroke it.*
>
> ▶ *If there's a tree or some long grass feel it with your hand.*

DON'T PLAY MIND GAMES

Now let's turn to the second lesson you've learned from your pet. Dogs don't play mind games – and nor do other animals. Of course, they like games of the stick-throwing kind and the rolling about kind. But dogs and animals don't play games of the 'I'll pretend I'm not pleased to see him' kind. They're honest and straightforward.

They're also uninhibited. Inhibition is a special involuntary kind of game playing and it's one of the great enemies of meaningful relationships and, therefore, of happiness. Inhibitions make us hide part of ourselves away, so we can't fully give ourselves to our friends, relatives and partners. Our inhibitions inhibit others. Our inhibitions make other people think they're seeing reality when, in fact, they're seeing an illusion. Our inhibitions make liars of us. We pretend we're being honest but we're not.

What we're all seeking is more meaningful contact. We want to engage with other people at a profound level. Talking about the weather hardly constitutes a meaningful engagement. If anything, it's the reverse. It's saying: 'You're not close to me; you're only permitted to talk to me about superficial things.'

So instead of talking about the weather, try talking about things that are more personal and profound – happiness, for example. Or coping with illness or disability. Or dealing with redundancy.

LEARN TO 'SEE' EMOTIONS

The third lesson you can learn from your pet is the visibility of emotions that we discussed above. Of course, you already have a limited ability to 'see' emotions and so does everybody else. But you can develop things much further. If you want to get on well with other people you have to push your happiness and your love ahead of you so they can easily see it.

You won't be able to push that aura ahead of you if you're a judgemental sort of person. Don't approach others with a feeling of hostility or suspicion, with your positive emotions hidden away behind your back like some precious metal. Other people will sense it.

Insight
One way of signalling your empathy with others is by matching their body language. Don't make this too deliberate or obvious or it will simply come across as artificial and insincere, the opposite of the intended effect. Rather, note when people are, for example, leaning towards you; in that case, you lean forward as well. Or if they're resting their chin on their hand, you might do the same. Done subtly, this works at the subconscious level, making other people feel good about you.

Remember, you can't empathize fully if you're harsh on people who are different from you. For example, if you've never smoked you'll never understand someone who's addicted to nicotine unless you seek to understand it non-judgementally. Nor, unless you're open-minded, will you be able to relate to people from different social backgrounds, different cultures or different age groups. Obviously, you'll widen your circle of friends if you can understand those differences.

- ▶ *Be interested in other people.*

- ▶ *Be compassionate towards other people.*

- ▶ *Be responsive – use facial expressions and tone of voice.*

- ▶ *Trust people with small things and work up to big things – don't distrust people without reason.*

- ▶ *Don't be judgemental.*

- ▶ *Try to find something you agree with.*

- ▶ *If you disagree, mention the thing you agree with before mentioning the thing you disagree with.*

Insight

If you confine your friendships to people with exactly the same background and outlook as yourself then, yes, things will be comfortable and easy. But you'll be limiting your opportunities for growth, new experiences and happiness if you do. And there's one kind of difference most of us are anxious to bridge – the one between the sexes.

Try this

Read this passage about Ernest Hemingway and then try to pump up your aura in the same way.

Something played off him – he was intense, electrokinetic, but in control, a racehorse reined in. He stopped to talk to one of the musicians in fluent Spanish and something about him hit me – enjoyment: God, I thought, how he's enjoying himself! I had never seen anyone with such an aura of fun and wellbeing. He radiated it and everyone in the place responded.

A. E. Hotchner writing about his first encounter with the American novelist
Ernest Hemingway

Living with 'the one'

I am in love – and, my God, it is the greatest thing that can happen to a man. I tell you, find a woman you can fall in love with. Do it. Let yourself fall in love. If you have not done so already, you are wasting your life.

D. H. Lawrence (1885–1930), English novelist

Will you be happier if you and your partner separate? It may seem an odd question with which to begin a section on love. But let's get it out of the way now. Because a recent study has shown that when a relationship is unhappy, men and women benefit equally by splitting up. If you're not going to split up, the alternative – the only alternative – is to stay together and make your relationship happy. There is no middle way on this one. Staying together and being unhappy or less than happy is not what you got together for.

It's your right to be happy. And, never forget, it's your partner's, too. So which is it? Are you separating or are you staying together? Make your choice. If you don't have the same goals, if you don't want the same kind of life, if you're not travelling in the same direction, if you stifle one-another's creativity rather than enhance it, then you're probably not going to be happy, whatever you do.

Love does not consist in gazing at each other, but in looking outward together in the same direction.

Antoine de Saint-Exupery (1900–44), French author and pilot

If you've plumped for staying together, read on. You've just committed yourself to building a relationship that makes both of you very happy. And one of the most important ways to do that is to learn something new and wonderful about your partner, yourself and your relationship every day.

One might compare two human beings to two bodies charged with electricity of different potentials. Isolated from each other the electric forces within them are invisible, but if they come into the right juxtaposition the force is transmuted, and a spark, a glow of burning light, arise between them. Such is love.

Marie Stopes (1880–1958), Scottish birth control campaigner

Avoid the projection trap

Don't copy D. H. Lawrence, whose enthusiastic view of relationships I quoted earlier. Lawrence fell for Frieda Weekley, who became the model and inspiration for so many of the female characters in his novels. She left a home, a husband and three young children to be with him. He called her 'the woman of a lifetime'.

Before long, they were battering one another.

Lawrence made a well-known mistake. He projected onto Frieda the fantasies he wanted to believe in. Remarkable though she was, she was never going to be able to live up to them. Frieda equally projected onto Lawrence her fantasies about great writers. Artistically it was a fruitful combination and it had its heights. But 'happy' is not the word for the relationship.

Happiness comes from discovering a reality much more interesting than anything you could have imagined. If you and your partner have been 'projecting', then, at some point, you're going to come down to earth with a bump. It's why, sooner or later, scientists say that the 'walking on air' feeling just can't last. The most cynical give it just a few weeks. None of them give it more than two years. But they're wrong. And I'll explain how to prove them wrong in a moment.

Keep smiling

Three reasons it's best to be the man in a heterosexual relationship:

▶ *Your name is yours forever.*
▶ *Your partner doesn't stare at your chest all the time you're talking to her.*
▶ *You can never get pregnant.*

And three reasons it's best to be the woman:

▶ *If the person you're going out with is better than you at something, you don't have to break up.*
▶ *You and your friends don't have to get drunk before you can share your feelings.*
▶ *You can wear your partner's clothes without being thought weird.*

There's another kind of projection, and that's projecting onto the relationship. The composer Wagner provides a pretty good example. This is what he wrote to his fellow composer Liszt: 'As I have never in my life known the real and true joy of love, I will raise a monument to that most beautiful of dreams in which, from beginning to end, this love is truly and entirely fulfilled.' The monument was his most passionate opera in which Isolde literally dies of love on the corpse of Tristan.

It's a beautiful vision in a way. Rather unromantically, psychologists call it the 'collapse of ego boundaries'. The two had become one in life. And in Wagner's extreme fantasy they also had to be one in death. But having a woman, as it were, dying of love on a daily basis doesn't get, say, the kids bathed. Wagner wouldn't have known true love if he was staring it in the face because he was looking for the wrong signs. That was his problem. He didn't realize that getting the shopping was love. He was too caught up in a world of myths and make-believe, as well as his own megalomania.

Love, and you shall be loved.

Ralph Waldo Emerson (1803–82), American philosopher and poet

Rules for walking on air

As we've already seen, that 'walking on air' feeling comes from the chemical PEA, of which we get a huge hit in the early days of a relationship. Admittedly, you'll never again quite achieve those levels, even using the additional techniques we've discussed in the chapters on eating and exercise, because there's an element that comes with novelty. But you can stay high all your life if you follow these rules.

FOUR KINDS OF ACCEPTANCE

▶ **Rule number 1.** *Accept your partner's love. You don't, like Wagner, insist it has to be expressed in a particular way. You have to be free to express your love your way and your partner has to be free to do the same. Simply enjoy the love. Bathe in it. Be grateful for it, because it's a wonderful thing.*

▶ **Rule number 2.** *Accept the way your partner is. You don't, like D. H. Lawrence, tell your partner how to dress or behave or what to think or, indeed, anything else. In other words, you don't project your fantasies onto your partner.*

▶ **Rule number 3.** *Accept your partner's growth. You don't try to keep your partner the way he/she was right back at the beginning* *of the relationship. You both have to be free to develop. In fact, learn to love change. Because if there was no change there could be no improvement. Would you, at, say, age 40, really want your partner to be the same as when you first met 20 years earlier? Not to know any more? Not to have acquired any more skills? Not to have more insight and wisdom?*

▶ **Rule number 4.** *Accept that two people are different and always will be (especially if one is a man and the other a woman). You already love some of the differences. Learn to love all of them.*

Try this

Draw a line down the middle of some sheets of paper from top to bottom. On the left, make a list of all the differences you have with your partner. On the right, set out all the things that are puzzling about those differences but also all the things that are wonderful about them. Have your partner do the same. Then discuss what you've written.

Problem: If I'm going to 'accept' everything I might just as well live with the first person who comes along

That's not what 'acceptance' is about. Acceptance means being in love with the way a person really is, not with the way you'd like that person to be.

NINE FURTHER RULES

▶ **Rule number 5.** *Always remain curious. Your partner is actually an inexhaustible mine. You'll never run out of treasures as long as you keep digging new galleries.*

▶ **Rule number 6.** *Always give support. Support is very important for both sexes but especially for women who have a strong need to be able to talk about themselves and their problems. In one study, 41 per cent of women who suffered a 'stressful life event' became depressed if they were given only a low level of support by their partners, but the figure fell to 10 per cent with a high level of support. Another study found that relationships in which partners react enthusiastically to one-another's good news are the happiest; don't be grudging or uninterested.*

▶ **Rule number 7.** *Always build your partner up. We've already seen how damaging negative thoughts and emotions can be. If you foster them in your partner – possibly as a way of gaining dominance in the relationship – you'll end up destroying him or her. Don't criticize and, above all, never make personal attacks.*

▶ **Rule number 8.** *Talk, talk, talk – and make it meaningful. One study found that talking to a woman is more meaningful than talking to a man. Both men and women reported that talking to a woman resulted in a conversation that was pleasanter, more intimate and – this is very important – with more self-disclosure. If you're a man, learn to be meaningful.*

▶ **Rule number 9.** *Don't make comparisons (see Chapter 3). Don't say or even think: 'He/She earns more money than my partner.'*

▶ **Rule number 10.** *Don't hold onto negative thoughts or emotions (see Chapters 3 and 4).*

▶ **Rule number 11.** *Provide plenty of physical contact. As we saw earlier, oxytocin is essential to your health as well as the health of your relationship.*

▶ **Rule number 12.** *Have plenty of sex. Sex is the source of several 'happy chemicals'. One study found that satisfaction with a relationship correlates very closely with frequency of intercourse minus the number of rows. Sex is dealt with in the next chapter.*

▶ **Rule number 13.** *Do something happy together every day.*

10 THINGS TO REMEMBER

1 *Relationships are the single most important source of human happiness.*

2 *If you're lonely, consider getting a pet; if you're not lonely, still consider getting a pet – stroking a pet reduces stress and improves health.*

3 *Love people the way you love your pet – unconditionally.*

4 *Oxytocin binds you to other people – the more touching, the more bonding.*

5 *Don't 'play games' in your relationship.*

6 *Push your love and happiness ahead of you so everyone can feel it.*

7 *Don't be judgemental.*

8 *Resolve to make your relationship happy – there's no middle way between that and separation.*

9 *The union of two people involving 'the collapse of ego boundaries' is the greatest happiness.*

10 *Don't project your fantasies onto your partner but love the reality; acceptance is the key to a happy relationship.*

HOW HAPPY ARE YOU NOW?

Have you been able to improve any relationships and, if so, have they in turn increased your happiness?

a *Yes.*
b *No, relationships are just the same.*
c *No, I'm all alone, though I don't want to be.*

If you answered '(a)' you're ready to move on to the next chapter. If you answered '(b)', read through this chapter again and try following all those 13 rules to see what develops. It's also worth looking again at Chapters 2 and 3. Some of the negative styles of thinking described there are as relevant to relationships as to other kinds of situations. Are you comparing, for example? (His wife is more fun.) Are you demanding more and more? (He just doesn't show as much affection as I need.) Are you insisting on perfection? (Why can't he dress more stylishly?) Are you using labels? (Mean uncle Bert.) If you answered '(c)' then, for the moment, you have to cultivate other sources of happiness. That's a useful skill, because we're all going to find ourselves alone at some time. Try to look at this period as a positive learning opportunity. It need not last long. There's a world full of people actively looking for friendship and love, just as you are. You might also like to read *Teach Yourself Confidence and Social Skills*. On the website you'll find details of social networking sites and internet dating agencies that could be useful.

Keep smiling

The teacher puts a sentence on the blackboard and asks the class to punctuate it correctly.

The boys do it like this: 'Woman, without her man, is nothing.'

The girls do it like this: 'Woman: without her, man is nothing.'

10

Happy sex

In this chapter you will learn:
- *why sex is the most important activity for happiness*
- *why getting rid of inhibitions is essential for happy sex*
- *how chemicals released during sex make us happy*
- *which techniques produce the maximum happiness.*

> *Praise be to God who has placed the source of man's greatest*
> *pleasure in woman's natural parts, and woman's greatest*
> *pleasure in the natural parts of man!*
>
> The Perfumed Garden

If you have a partner, sex is the most wonderful thing you can do together to create happiness. Some people talk of 'just sex'. If this includes you then, quite honestly, you haven't yet experienced sex to the full, which means you have something marvellous to look forward to.

Never think in terms of 'just sex'. It would be like saying 'just love' or describing the Milky Way as 'just a load of gas' or Rodin's sculptures as 'just a pile of minerals'. 'Just sex' exists but that's not what we're concerned with here. We're talking about sex as the thrilling, endlessly fascinating and incredibly beautiful way two souls unite and, in uniting, discover they're also united with the whole universe, which is going to make you feel very happy indeed.

Just so you don't think I'm only speaking for myself, I'm enlisting the help of some scientists and statisticians. In 2003, five researchers asked 1,000 *women* to rate 19 activities in terms of the happiness they produced. Sex was rated the activity that produces the single largest amount of happiness.

I've italicized 'women' to emphasize that it's not only men, as some would have us believe, who think that sex produces happiness. (And if you want to know what came bottom of the list it was commuting to and from work.)

The point is reinforced by Andrew Oswald, Professor of Economics at Warwick University in the UK and David Blanchflower of Dartmouth College in the USA. They analysed data on 16,000 adult Americans and concluded: 'There is little evidence… that men enjoy sex slightly more than women.' This is a rather lukewarm way of saying that sex makes men and women equally happy.

Oswald and Blanchflower's next conclusion is even more important. They didn't pin down exactly the optimum amount but, in their almost unfathomable statistical way, observed that: 'Having sex at least four times a week is associated with approximately 0.12 happiness points.' These rather obscure-sounding 'happiness points' are actually highly significant. In clearer language the researchers had this to say: 'The more sex, the happier the person.'

Very significantly they also noted that: 'Celibacy and small amounts of sex have statistically indistinguishable effects upon happiness.' In other words, a lot of sex produces a lot of happiness but a little sex produces almost none.

It seems, however, that very few people actually know what makes them happy (see Chapter 8) because only around 7 per cent of Americans reported having sex four times a week or more.

Let's turn from the scientists to the poets. Shelley defined love as 'the universal thirst for a communion not merely of the senses, but of our whole nature, intellectual, imaginative and sensitive…'. He then went on to define the role of sex in the following terms: 'The sexual impulse, which is only one, and often a small part of those claims, serves, from its obvious and external nature, as a kind of expression of the rest.'

In other words, sex can be communion on every level; total union; the end of separation; a oneness; the end of loneliness; happiness.

The elements of happy sex

The kind of sex that I'm talking about has several elements, of which the most important are:

▶ *love*
▶ *monogamy*
▶ *absence of inhibition*
▶ *spirituality*
▶ *frequency*.

LOVE AND MONOGAMY

Most people can enjoy sex without being in love. And sex between freely consenting adults who are not in love is, for many people, far better than no sex at all. But the optimum sex, the kind of sex I want to deal with here, can only be achieved by two people who love one another.

To back me up I'm once again going to turn to the scientists. Oswald and Blanchflower found that, in the course of a year, the number of sexual partners for maximum happiness is one. That's right – one. (And if they'd asked not about the past year but the past five or ten or 20 years they would have got the same result.) People who had sex outside of their marriages had low happiness scores and so did those who had ever paid for sex. So, there's no need to feel jealous of rock stars who report having had sex with hundreds or even thousands of partners. It may or may not thrill a particular individual to behave like that but, for most people, it's not the way to happiness.

Insight

We don't have to look very far for an explanation. Ultimate sex, as Shelley observed, involves communion on every level. But if you're not in love you won't be fully open to your partner on any of those levels, not even the purely physical.

ABSENCE OF INHIBITION

We've already talked about inhibition in the context of 'being yourself' (Chapter 8). It's especially important when it comes to sex. The fact that you're in love doesn't by any means guarantee that your sex life, or any other part of your life together, will be uninhibited. But unless you're uninhibited, communion on every level can't take place.

The fact is that even nowadays, despite all the media exposure to sexual images and all the talk of sexual liberation, many people are still frightened of sex. If you feel the need to drink alcohol in order to have sex then this includes you.

Fear and guilt about sex have their origins in childhood. Parents don't want their children experimenting with sex at too young an age and they often use fear as a way of deterring them. Even saying nothing at all about sex is a kind of disapproving comment. And many parents who don't normally want to discuss sex with their children will nevertheless take the opportunity of, say, a sex scene in a film to give their views on 'immoral' behaviour and the risks of sexually transmitted diseases and unwanted pregnancies.

It's very rare for parents to talk about sex in a positive way. In fact, it's rare for anybody to talk about sex in a positive way. Even sex educators tend to concentrate on the perils of sex rather than its pleasures. So it's no surprise that it can take years or even decades to overcome our inhibitions (meanwhile, perhaps, passing them on to the next generation). I'll have more to say about this in a moment.

SPIRITUALITY

Sex won't be fully rewarding unless it involves a spiritual element. That's to say, communion on far more than a purely physical level. When spirituality enters the picture you feel that you're making contact with the secret essence of your partner, that the physical boundary between you and your partner no longer exists, nor that between the two of you and the rest of the universe.

Using sexual energy for spirituality is known as tantric sex. It's dealt with in more detail below.

> *The more sensitive, the more romantic, and the more idealistic is the young person of either sex, the more his or her soul craves for some kindred soul with whom the whole being can unite.*
>
> Marie Stopes (1880–1958), Scottish birth control campaigner

FREQUENCY

Most couples don't have sex often enough to enjoy the full benefits. According to Oswald and Blanchflower, couples should cuddle naked every day and, as discussed above, aim for intercourse at least four times a week.

How does sex make you happy?

However ecstatic sex may make you feel at the time, can it fundamentally alter your level of happiness the other, shall we say, 163 hours of the week? The answer is that, yes, sex can make you feel happy both at the time and for a while afterwards. One of the reasons is that sex increases the level of certain 'happy' chemicals in the body. Do it often enough and the effect will never leave you.

> ▶ *Dopamine – this is the neurotransmitter that makes sex and everything else that's pleasurable, pleasurable. Without it, you wouldn't have the motivation to get out of bed in the morning. With it, you can't wait to get back into bed. Dopamine increases sex and sex increases dopamine. It's what makes you feel ecstasy and rapture. A beneficial side effect is that when your dopamine is high from sex you won't be so interested in drugs or alcohol.*
> ▶ *PEA (phenylethylamine) – this is the chemical that produces that 'walking on air' feeling. It's an amphetamine-like substance that stimulates dopamine and is naturally high in the early days of a love affair. If you want to keep it high throughout your relationship then have plenty of sex, because it peaks at orgasm.*
> ▶ *Oxytocin – when you enjoy oxytocin together with someone else you're bonded. You're far more likely to stay together and you're far more likely to forget previous partners. If you want your relationship to endure you want oxytocin. And how do you get it? By touching and particularly by having plenty of sex because it also peaks at orgasm. Like PEA, oxytocin increases dopamine, too.*

You can see that these three chemicals together can create an extremely potent 'happy' cocktail. There's one other vital element: semen makes women happy. At first, it may sound ridiculous. But there's good scientific evidence for it. And even before there was scientific evidence, many sexual philosophers have believed it going back hundreds and even thousands of years. In fact, the mingling of male and female 'essences' is fundamental to the Chinese philosophy of Taoism. If you've heard of yin and yang then you've already got an understanding of it. Yin is the female principle and yang is the male principle. The two have to be in harmony in both men and women, as well as throughout the universe.

In Taoist thought, that harmony can be brought about during sex, when not only can a woman absorb a man's yang essences (now proven) but a man can absorb a woman's yin essences (not proven, to my knowledge). It's fascinating to reflect that the Taoists already held these beliefs more than two millennia ago. In the West they're more recent but they have pedigree. Marie Stopes, whose name endures through the clinics she set up, wrote the same in her wonderful book *Married Love*, published in 1918.

So what is this proof? A team led by Gordon Gallup, a psychologist at the State University of New York, looked for a relationship between the sex lives of women and their degree of happiness, using the Beck Depression Inventory (a standard questionnaire for assessing mood). The team discovered that women whose partners never used condoms were significantly happier than women whose partners always or usually used condoms. The unhappiest were the women who weren't having any sex at all.

After controlling for various factors, Gallup and his team concluded that the happiest women were, indeed, absorbing 'happy' chemicals from their partners' semen through the walls of their vaginas. This is not so very surprising in fact, because semen contains various mood-altering hormones including testosterone, oestrogen, follicle-stimulating hormone, luteinizing hormone, prolactin and several prostaglandins. Some of these chemicals from the partners have been detected in women's bloodstreams soon after sex.

Warning

Sexually transmitted diseases and unwanted pregnancies would more than offset any of the psychological benefits of semen. If you need to use condoms then you should continue to do so.

How to have happy sex

You now know about some of the 'sex chemicals' involved in happiness. How can you have sex so as to optimize those chemicals and, therefore, happiness?

RULE NUMBER 1: LOTS OF CUDDLING

Oxytocin, as we've seen, is a very desirable chemical. The way to optimize it is to touch as often and as completely as possible. Sleep naked and start every day with a naked cuddle. Use every opportunity you can. Cuddling shouldn't only be a prelude to sex. It's something very important in its own right.

> ## Try this
> ▶ *Spooning. A lovely position to adopt when you're naked in bed together, drifting off to sleep or slowly waking up. You lay on your sides, facing the same way, nicely relaxed and pressed together.*
> ▶ *Whole body embrace. This is the best way of maximizing contact. You lay one on top of the other, face to face. Your feet should touch.*
> ▶ *The armchair. A great position when you both want to read or watch television. One of you sits on the floor or bed, legs apart, to make a kind of armchair, and the other sits between the legs, facing the same direction.*
> ▶ *The sitting embrace. When you want to talk, or share a drink, or feed one another appetizers, this is how you do it. One of you sits on the floor or bed cross-legged and the other sits on the first one's lap, facing.*

RULE NUMBER 2: SELF-EXPRESSION

In Chapter 8 we looked at the importance of self-expression. Well, this applies just as much to sex as to everything else. If you're afraid of the consequences of your own self-expression, or your partner's, don't be. On the contrary, self-expression is liberating and your relationship will be all the better for it. You'll be happier.

As regards sexual techniques, there are bound to be things you'd like to do sexually that you and your partner haven't done before. This can be delicate. Of course, when passion takes over, it's normal to explore new territory without consciously thinking about it and your partner may equally be carried along. It could be that your partner wants to try these things as well and has been waiting for you to take the lead. But it isn't fair to try to do something you know your partner isn't happy with. Discussion and compromise are the ways forward.

Fantasies can be a problem area. We all have sexual fantasies. The question is how much you should tell your partner. Well, ideally you should be able to reveal all your sexual fantasies and your partner should be able to do likewise. After all, your fantasies, sexual or otherwise, are part of your personality. If you feel you have to hide your fantasies from your partner then you're not free and you can't be fully happy.

One of the fears is that fantasies reflect genuine desires. Relax. Most sexual fantasies couldn't come true, anyway. They tend to involve people with perfect bodies who behave exactly as the fantasist wants. They don't have any sexually transmitted diseases or body odour. They're never jealous or shy or inhibited. And so on.

On the other hand, you might fantasize about things that are perfectly possible and you might go on to try them, if that's what you both want.

Generally speaking, the least threatening and most common fantasies are those that only involve the two of you exploring new techniques or places to make love. Going a little further, some people are excited by the idea of an audience. Typical examples are being on display, being filmed naked or people watching while you make love.

You may be on slightly more delicate ground if you introduce the idea of a third person in the lovemaking. Or, who knows, it may not be delicate ground at all. You might suggest: 'You're so sexy you really need two women/two men to pleasure you.'
Or: 'Last night I dreamed I was in a harem.'

Some couples stick to fantasy characters. Others might refer to actual people who are friends or acquaintances, which certainly carries a greater risk of creating jealousies.

Insight

So couldn't fantasies be a source of unhappiness rather than happiness? Well, of course they could. As I said at the beginning, sharing fantasies is an ideal but it's one you might not be able to fully attain.

Try this

▶ *Express your artistic side. Take turns to choose the ambience, so you both get the chance to express your personalities. Flowers, perfumes, incense, music (see later), the colour and material of the sheets, mood lighting, candles... Why not go even further? Say, a four-poster bed, mirrors, Arabian-style drapes as if you're in a tent in the desert, sound effects, a striptease dance...*
▶ *Get rid of inhibitions. It's important to make a conscious decision to fight inhibition. The journey can be a long one but it's extremely interesting. And every step forward brings a reward. Buy a sex manual (there are suggestions at the back of the book) and both read it. Make a list of the things you'd like to try. Then agree you'll set aside, say, one session a month for experimentation. That way, neither of you is under any pressure on the other occasions. There's no need to be in a rush. Don't be despondent if your partner is more inhibited than you are. On the other hand, don't be defensive if your partner is more adventurous than you are. Just take things slowly, one step at a time. If one of you*
(Contd)

> *tries to hurry things, the other may get frightened, which*
> *would be a shame. If you're the inhibited one, try using*
> *visualization during meditation (Chapter 6) to get used to*
> *new ideas.*
> ▶ *Fantasies. If you want to tease out your partner's fantasies,*
> *and reveal your own, just hint at something when you're*
> *having sex and see what your partner's reaction is. If your*
> *partner tenses up and doesn't respond you may well be on*
> *the wrong track. It certainly doesn't mean your partner isn't*
> *interested in any sexual fantasies at all. Maybe you just got*
> *the wrong one. Don't press it for now. Try something else a*
> *few days later.*

RULE NUMBER 3: MUSIC

Dr Johnson called music the only sensual pleasure without
vice. Shakespeare called it the food of love. If it's fast and
furious, sex is fast and furious. If it's languid, sex is languid.
Music has a powerful effect on us even if we're not consciously
aware of it.

Without any doubt, music is the most mysterious of the arts,
working in ways that still aren't completely understood. But we
know that when a piece of music gives you that 'funny feeling'
it's stimulating the reward structures of the brain. In other words,
music can go as directly to your brain as a recreational drug and,
indeed, some cultures have deplored it for that very reason. At
the same time, activity in the amygdala is inhibited. That's the
part of the brain associated with fear. So music can make you
feel confident – always a good thing where sex is concerned – and
augment arousal. It's indispensable.

If you want proof, scientists have found that music we like
tends to:

▶ *lower cortisol, the stress hormone*
▶ *lower testosterone, a hormone which can cause irritability*
  and aggression

- *increase oxytocin, the 'touch' hormone*
- *increase endorphins, the body's painkillers.*

Lower cortisol reduces anxiety, including performance anxiety, so that's a good thing. Lower testosterone may sound like a bad thing where sex is concerned. But testosterone seems more related to desire than function and, since you've already got the desire when you put the music on, there shouldn't be a problem. However, it seems that some music may increase testosterone – if you feel the need for more testosterone, go for something a little more aggressive. Higher oxytocin will increase skin sensation, including the genitals. It also increases dopamine and serotonin. Throw in increased endorphins and you're headed for a big high.

> ### Try this
> **Select several quite different pieces of music.** Make love to each of them for a few minutes. How did they influence what you did and what you felt?

RULE NUMBER 4: MULTIPLE ORGASMS FOR WOMEN

Years ago women didn't have orgasms because they didn't expect to have orgasms (nor did their partners expect them to). Now, the majority of women have one orgasm because they expect to have just one orgasm. Some of them, it has to be said, are completely satisfied by their single orgasm and that's fine. But the more orgasms you have then (within reason) the more of those 'happy chemicals' you'll enjoy.

The way to unlock your multi-orgasmic capacity is not through intercourse but through masturbation. Have your one orgasm by your usual solo method. But don't have it in the back of your mind that you'll settle for one. Be optimistic. Now simply continue to play with your clitoris. It may well be that you'll surprise yourself by having a second orgasm without doing anything else, and a third. If not, you're going to have to do something unusual, something extra, to get those additional orgasms.

Try this

- *Put on some sensual, very rhythmical music.*
- *Strip completely naked, if you're not already.*
- *Relax. Give yourself an hour to succeed.*
- *Rub yourself all over with some body oil.*
- *Stimulate other places in addition to your clitoris – the entrance to your vagina, your G-spot area, your anus, your nipples… whatever excites you.*
- *Use a vibrator.*
- *Try watching an erotic video or DVD or yourself in a mirror.*
- *Increase the blood flow by spanking yourself.*
- *Try different positions. On your back, open your legs as far as you can or, alternatively, press them hard together with the vibrator between your thighs and against your vulva. Or try kneeling with your thighs open and lean back as far as you can – use some pillows to support you. The more physical tension you create the better.*
- *Use fantasy.*
- *Speak your fantasy out loud.*
- *Focus.*
- *Make plenty of noise.*

RULE NUMBER 5: SIMULTANEOUS ORGASMS

Simultaneous orgasms go in and out of fashion as the apogee of great sex. But where happy sex is concerned they're always a very good idea. The ideal is for a woman to have several orgasms before the man has his and then to have one 'big one' together. This brings the active stage of lovemaking to an end and you can then both fully luxuriate in that wonderful glow.

Insight

Although most couples find simultaneous orgasms hugely satisfying there is a technique that comes under the heading of tantric sex, by which the man does *not* ejaculate. Nevertheless, the woman can enjoy multiple orgasms and the man a whole series of 'mini-orgasms', leaving both of you very happy indeed. The technique is explained below.

RULE NUMBER 6: AVOIDING THE SEXUAL HANGOVER – MULTIPLE ORGASMS FOR MEN

So far I've talked of sex unreservedly as a generator of happiness. But the chemical changes in the body following sex can sometimes send you down rather than up. This happens to men far more than women and to older men far more than younger men. It comes about most of all when men ejaculate too much as excess ejaculation leads to depletion of serotonin.

Serotonin, you may remember, is a chemical that helps make us feel contented. Other chemicals are involved as well but, for sure, if we don't have enough serotonin we're liable to feel anxious and aggressive. Some researchers gave the serotonin-lowering drug PCPA to animals and were horrified by the results. The animals began torturing and eating their partners while mating.

In humans it's known that young men are more likely to commit crimes after sex. And older men sometimes feel depressed after sex. It's this that's known as the sexual hangover and, apart from anything else, it spoils the post-sex period for hours or even days.

From the point of view of the sexual hangover, how much ejaculation is too much? A simple test is this: do you feel glowing, elated and happy after ejaculation or slightly lower than you were? If it's the latter then you're ejaculating too often.

Insight

Every man is different, but as a rough guide think in terms of three ejaculations a week in youth, once a week in middle age and once a month in old age.

But there seems to be a paradox here. How can you have sex frequently enough to make both of you happy, and yet without the man ejaculating so often that he gets a hangover? The solution is actually very simple. Some of the time the man has sex without ejaculating.

It's this that's known as 'multiple orgasms for men'. If you're puzzled by this because you think orgasm and ejaculation are one and the same thing then let me explain. The word 'ejaculation' covers the emission of fluid. The word 'orgasm' covers the highly pleasurable muscular contractions. Normally the two go together. But you can learn to orgasm without ejaculating.

Having multiple orgasms doesn't mean having several of the kind of orgasm you have now. They are totally different. Multiple orgasms for men are both less and more than the normal kind.

Here's how they're more:

▶ *You won't suffer the sexual hangover.*
▶ *You can prolong lovemaking.*
▶ *You won't lose your sexual vitality in the way you do with 'ordinary' sex.*
▶ *You and your partner can have sex more often – once a day, for example, or even several times a day.*
▶ *Your hormone balance will be different – you'll feel more affectionate and loving.*

- *You'll feel 'mystical'.*
- *You'll never be afraid of not being able to perform.*

And here's how they're less:

- *You'll feel less physical sensation than when ejaculation and orgasm are combined.*

Insight

Put like that, multiple orgasms may not sound very appealing, however long the list of advantages. But, in the brain, multiple orgasms are exquisite. Once you become good at the technique, you'll find that each is more powerful than the previous one. Eventually you'll reach a state of ecstasy.

So how can you experience these multiple orgasms?

Different sexologists describe different methods. One involves strengthening a muscle known as the PC muscle until it can actually shut off the ejaculation. Another involves pressing a special point (the 'Million dollar point') between the testicles and the anus. And there are still others.

I'm not going to describe any of these physical techniques. Some require months of training, some interfere too much with lovemaking, some are painful and some don't work. Instead, I'm going to describe a very simple technique that requires nothing other than the power of your mind, which is considerable.

Try this
The first step is to practise the technique during masturbation.
Probably you already use stop/go as a way of prolonging your pleasure. That simply means that you stop stimulating yourself once you get 'too' excited, let your erection subside a little, then begin again. For multiple orgasms you simply have to refine that technique so you can get closer and closer to the point of no return without 'going over the edge' into ejaculation.

(Contd)

In order to experience orgasm without ejaculation you have to get very, very close indeed. At the critical moment you have to cease physical and mental stimulation instantly:

- *Stop stroking your penis.*
- *Stop thrusting movements.*
- *Stop all muscle tension (for example, lower your legs if they're in the air).*
- *Stop breathing or, alternatively, pant (experiment to see what works best for you).*
- *Stop fantasizing (if you were).*
- *Stop looking at sexy images (if you were).*
- *Stop 'talking dirty' (if you were).*
- *Stop concentrating on the sensations.*

In other words, you have to turn off like a light. Once you've achieved multiple orgasms solo you can start employing the technique with your partner.

Insight

Don't be surprised if you don't experience much excitement from your first partial orgasm. It doesn't mean you've done anything 'wrong'. The second will be better. The third better still. Eventually, you'll experience sensations that'll be almost unbearably exquisite.

Problem: If I don't ejaculate, won't my partner be denied the 'happy chemicals' in my semen?

The scientists haven't looked at this as far as I know but, in reality, a certain amount of fluid always 'leaks' from the penis during multiple orgasms so some 'happy chemicals' should still get through.

RULE NUMBER 7: TANTRIC (OR SACRED) SEX

This is the most important rule and, now that you've mastered the previous six, you're ready for it. The pop star Sting has become famous for his five-hour tantric sex sessions. But tantric sex is not primarily about numbers of hours. It's about using sexual energy for spiritual purposes. Of course, that's not to say you'll want to have this style of sex every time. But, when you do, it will take you to a whole new higher plane of happiness.

Nobody knows for sure how or when tantra arose but it was probably in India more than 2,000 years ago. It certainly ties in with Hindu belief about the origin of the visible universe as described in the Vedas, which is that, at one time, there was neither what is, nor what is not. In the infinite peace the ONE was breathing. For convenience, the ONE is pictured as a male god and given the name Shiva. Shiva was lonely so created Shakti, the female. At that moment, the visible universe came into being, composed of opposites, male and female, positive and negative, matter and anti-matter and so on.

Sex was just one aspect of tantra, not the whole of it as many people think. It was – and is – the reuniting of the male and female so as to experience the Divine Consciousness. The sensations of sex were believed to be a foretaste of the infinite joy that would be experienced by those who eventually escaped 'the cycle of death and rebirth'.

Recently, tantric sex has been adopted in the West and changed out of all recognition. Almost anything that has to do with a more gentle, considerate, imaginative – and lengthy – style of sex is now given the tantric tag. But this completely misses the point. Tantric sex is not about particular techniques but about spirituality. If a spiritual experience is the aim then the tantric tag is valid. Everything else is, well, not tantra.

> *Only when souls flowing together, acting as one, distinct in individuality, but united in their action are thus mated, are the psycho-physiological laws met and satisfied.*
>
> Alice Bunker Stockham (1833–1912), Amerian gynaecologist

So how do you go about building the spiritual element?

achieved during sex. As the sadhakas (followers of tantra) say: 'Spirit alone can know spirit.' Which brings us very neatly to the subject of the next chapter.

The modern, small-minded ascetic endeavours to grow spiritually by destroying his physical instincts instead of by using them. But I would proclaim that we are set in the world to mould matter that it may express our spirits.

Marie Stopes (1880–1958), Scottish birth control campaigner

10 THINGS TO REMEMBER

1 *Sex makes us all happy – men and women equally.*

2 *The optimum frequency for happiness seems to be four or more times a week.*

3 *Other key elements in happy sex are love, the absence of inhibition, spirituality and monogamy.*

4 *The people with the happiest sex lives are those who have had one partner during the previous year.*

5 *The body's own chemicals involved in making sex happy include dopamine, PEA and oxytocin.*

6 *Women can absorb 'happy chemicals' from semen through the walls of their vaginas.*

7 *The techniques of happy sex include plenty of cuddling, self-expression, music, multiple orgasms for women and simultaneous orgasms (except in tantric sex).*

8 *Simultaneous orgasms are easy to achieve once you've learned which of your partner's 'buttons' to press.*

9 *Men can suffer a 'sexual hangover' that spoils the post-sex happiness for both of you – the answer is to master the technique for multiple orgasms for men.*

10 *Tantric sex adds spirituality and takes lovemaking to a higher plane.*

HOW HAPPY ARE YOU NOW?

Would you say your sex life has improved and, if so, are you happier generally?

  a *Yes.*
  b *Yes, sex has improved but that doesn't make me any happier the rest of the time.*
  c *No, we're still not having very much sex.*
  d *No, I/we can't seem to manage these techniques.*

If you answered '(a)' move on to the next chapter. If you answered '(b)' because your sex life has improved but you're no happier generally, then it could be that you're still not having *enough* of the right kind of sex. Or, if you're a man, it could be you're ejaculating too *often*. Are you having some kind of sexual activity (not necessarily intercourse) every day? As regards ejaculation, read *Rule number 6* again and keep practising the technique for multiple orgasms.

If you answered '(c)' because you're not having sex very often there could be all kinds of reasons for that. Some general advice is to agree to give sex a higher priority as a trial, whether you feel like it or not. Many people, no matter how much they enjoy sex *when they're doing it*, don't feel a very strong drive the rest of the time (take another look at Chapter 8, especially the part about people not being very good at predicting what will make them happy). So it may be necessary to agree to have sex with a certain regularity, at least to see what happens. You don't wait until you're starving before you eat, so why should you wait until you're 'sex-starved' before you have sex?

If you answered '(d)' because you and your partner are having problems with the advanced techniques, don't let that become a source of anxiety. There's no rush to perfect these techniques. Enjoy the journey.

Keep smiling
  If love is blind, why is lingerie so popular?

11

....

Connection equals happiness

In this chapter you will learn:
- *why you're never really alone*
- *how Nature makes you happy*
- *how generosity makes you happy*
- *how to achieve bliss through a more spiritual style of meditation.*

> *He who wants to do good knocks at the gate; he who loves finds the gates open.*
>
> Sir Rabindranath Tagore (1861–1941), Bengali writer

> *When the power of love overcomes the love of power the world will know peace.*
>
> Jimi Hendrix (1942–70), American rock guitarist

No matter how happy all the things I've already described make you, there's always going to be a little 'hole' if you don't include spirituality. Human beings need spirituality. Spirituality has many definitions but I'm talking about your sense of connection with other things – with people you know, with people you don't know, with animals, with plants, with this planet, with this solar system, with the furthest reaches of the universe.

Let me ask you a question. If, somehow, you could know for a fact that there were people like you living on another planet a thousand light years away, would it make any difference to you? If it would, that's spirituality. The sense that you're connected to life, although no actual connection is apparent.

Two of the most famous words of the twentieth century were written by the novelist E. M. Forster: 'Only connect!' We all crave it. We all fear separation. Connection is happiness.

Problem: I'm an atheist

You don't have to be religious to be spiritual. Even the Dalai Lama, the Buddhist spiritual leader of the Tibetan people, recognizes as much. 'I believe,' he says, 'that each individual should embark upon a spiritual path that is best suited to his or her mental disposition, natural inclination, temperament, belief, family and cultural background.'

In other words, you don't have to identify yourself as a Buddhist or a Christian or anything else – although, of course, you may.

All life is connected

The universe is a very, very strange place. As the biologist J. B. S. Haldane once observed: 'The universe is not only queerer than we suppose, it is queerer than we *can* suppose.' And the 'queerest' things of all are you, your dependence on everything else in the universe and your connection with them. In fact, you never can walk alone, even if you want to.

And I'm now going to prove it to you. Apart from anything else, you'll find it extremely difficult to be unhappy when you know these facts. You should feel exhilarated.

PROOF NUMBER 1

Everything, including the air, is made of atoms. Atoms are mostly composed of empty space – a nucleus circled at a vast distance (in relative terms) by one or more electrons. One analogy is that if the whole atom was enlarged to the size of the dome of St Paul's cathedral, the nucleus would only be the size of a grain of sand in the middle.

Since you're mostly empty space and everything else is mostly empty space, there's far less difference than you think between you and anything else. In other words, you're rather like a tornado in the air or a whirlpool in a river with things (nutrients, for example) constantly entering your vortex and leaving it.

The Great Oneness

There's evidence to suggest that newborn babies can't distinguish between themselves and anything else.
This leads to two interesting possibilities: one, the idea of merging with the 'Great Oneness' is nothing more than a desire to regress to that early infantile state; two, an infant is right to feel that sense of being at one with the universe because, actually, it is. It's we adults who have deluded ourselves that we're separate.

PROOF NUMBER 2

Every single atom of which you are composed came from the stars and has already been in millions of other organisms – because atoms can survive for a million years or more. A billion may well have been in Shakespeare or Boudicca (or any other historical figure you care to think of). Probably none of those atoms has been part of you for more than nine years and the vast majority won't form part of you for more than a month.

PROOF NUMBER 3

You have something like 10,000 trillion cells in your body and each cell has millions of components, including mitochondria, which are the cells' power stations. Way, way back in time mitochondria seem to have been bacteria, living quite separately and, even now, they have their own DNA, quite distinct from yours. This means that, in a manner of speaking, you're not a single organism but a whole collection of bacteria living in mutual dependence.

PROOF NUMBER 4

In 1997, scientists at the University of Geneva succeeded in separating a pair of sub-atomic particles and sending one in one direction and the other in the opposite direction. When the particles were seven miles apart, they changed the axis of one of the particles, and the other – in accordance with the predictions of quantum theory – changed its axis instantly. No one knows how.

To scientists this means that instead of the properties of systems being determined by the properties of the individual parts (the 'classical' view of physics), the properties of the parts are determined by the whole (the 'quantum' view of physics).

To philosophers it's proof that, in the words of one Buddhist sage: 'Things derive their being and nature by mutual dependence and are nothing in themselves.' Or in the words of the English metaphysical poet and preacher, John Donne: 'No man is an island, entire of itself.'

It also means there could be some way, after all, of communicating with those people on that distant planet.

> **What is now proved was once only imagin'd.**
>> William Blake (1757–1827), English poet and mystic

PROOF NUMBER 5

The psychologist, Carl Jung, noticed that certain symbols recurred throughout history in different societies all over the world, even those that had had no contact with one another. This, among other things, prompted him to develop the idea of the 'collective unconscious'. Inside us all are 'an untold abundance of images which have accumulated over millions of years of development'.

> ## Try this
> **Next time you're feeling overwhelmed by a problem, read the five proofs above.** They should help you get things into perspective.

CASE STUDY

Tricia's story

I know it sounds a bit crazy, but when I'm feeling down I put on some ethereal kind of music and look at my book of photographs taken by the Hubble Space Telescope. When I see the pictures of, say, the Andromeda Galaxy or the Whirlpool Galaxy M51, I'm absolutely overwhelmed by the beauty of it all. It never fails to make me feel blissfully happy.

Say 'hello' to your very big family

As we saw in Chapter 9, the more relatives you're close to the happier you're likely to be. Well, here's another amazing piece of 'queer' information. You've got billions of close relatives.

How? Because, according to many scientists, life on Earth successfully began just once. Think about it. It's staggering. If it's true it means – it's connection again – that every single living thing is directly related to every other living thing.

Let me elaborate. Back in the dawn of time (about 3.85 billion years ago, scientists think) all those primeval ponds were going 'glug glug glug'. It wouldn't have been unreasonable to assume that, when the conditions for life to arise were right, so indeed it would have happened in thousands of ponds all over the planet. But no, it happened, successfully anyway, in just one pond, at one moment, once only. And it never, ever happened again.

We're all – everything that lives – descendants of the same blob out of the same glug.

If you're a religious person you'll certainly find confirmation for your belief in the extraordinary probability that life successfully began on Earth only once. And that may certainly make you happy.

But even if you're an atheist, you can't fail to be moved by the knowledge that a tree is a relative of yours. Go and hug one right now. Your dog is a relative of yours. Go and pat him. The grass is a relative of yours. Go and lay on it. Even the tiniest creatures in the sea, as well as the largest, are relatives of yours. Go and swim with them.

This is true even if it turns out all life didn't come from the same blob. Because we know that any two human beings anywhere on the planet will, on average, have 99.9 per cent of their genes identical. With mice, you still share 90 per cent of your genes. Flies are 60 per cent the same. You even share genes with vegetables. I could go on. The point is that being in contact with Nature will make you happy because you're part of it.

If you live in the countryside, you've already got a head start. If you live in the town, especially if you don't have a garden, you'll need to make more of an effort. But wherever you live, get out and make the acquaintance of your relatives.

If that all sounds too mystical for your taste, bear this in mind. Human beings have been on the planet (depending on what you call a human being) for about 15 million years. And 99.9 per cent of that time has been spent living 'in nature'. Nowadays, most of us live in towns, but human beings didn't evolve to live in towns. Our way of living, our environment, has changed very fast, but we haven't changed at all. And we can't change. At least, not that quickly.

You're almost certainly living in a town. Most people are. And you may well say you like it. Love it, even. Tried the countryside and couldn't stand it. Couldn't abide the mud. But, then, why are you reading this book? I'll tell you why. Because there's a little void inside you that you can't ever seem to fill up. Am I right? And now you know one of the reasons. At the very least, the savannah, where humans lived for 2 million years, is imprinted in you. It's in your genes. That's why we all try to recreate the savannah in our gardens – open grassland, a few trees, a water feature. Fight it, if you insist, but that's not the way to happiness.

> ### Try this
> **Go out into the countryside and search for a landscape that 'speaks' to you. A place that seems special.** Then don't just look at it. Get in it – smell things, taste things, touch things, hug them. Get down on your hands and knees. Roll on the ground. If it's practical, take your clothes off – at least some. Get skin contact. Open your arms like a bird and 'glide' around. If there's water, swim naked. Feel how much you're a part of Nature and how right it is.

No noise on the savannah

There was little noise on the savannah. And when there was, it meant just one thing: danger! It still means the same to you today, even though you may not realize it. It's just one example of Nature inside you and the very physical effects of ignoring it.

You may think you're used to the noise of the city. But your body thinks otherwise. Tests on people who have lived in towns for years show they're still stressed by noise.

Even when you're asleep at night, your body is aware of noise. Occasional noise at night may mean nothing worse than fatigue in the morning. But years of noise mean:

▶ *higher levels of stress hormones in the blood, including cortisol*
▶ *higher levels of glucose, insulin, lipids and cholesterol in the blood*
▶ *higher loss of magnesium from cells*
▶ *increased heartbeat*
▶ *increased blood pressure*
▶ *decreased blood circulation to peripheral organs*
▶ *weakened immune system*
▶ *greater susceptibility to psychological problems.*

It's been calculated that the increased risk of damage to your health begins with night-time noise levels as low as 42 decibels (dB). At around 55 dB you have a 5 per cent increased probability of ill health and at 70 dB the probability goes up to more than 11 per cent. That's not even very loud. A nearby jackhammer, for example, would be 90 dB.

Noise is only one aspect of city life that opposes happiness. There are plenty of others, including the overcrowding, the pushing and shoving, that – paradoxically – leads to alienation from other people. The very opposite of the connection we're all trying to feel.

Altruism equals happiness

So I've proved to you that you're connected. So what? Well, quite a lot, actually. Apart from making you far less likely to feel lonely (which is already enormous), connection motivates you towards the happy state of altruism. Research shows that the happiest people are the ones who are doing something to make the world a better place. It doesn't seem to matter whether it's a big something or a small something, just as long as it's something.

It's not just a question of feeling good about yourself and what you're achieving, although, of course, these people do. It's also a question of taking control of your own life. When we do nothing, we feel like victims of outside forces which are, for example, destroying the rainforests, causing the extinction of whales, or bombing children. When we do something about it, we feel more at peace with ourselves.

Only a year before I met him, Richard (whom we encountered in Chapter 8) had tried to commit suicide. Very early one morning, he'd ridden his motorbike flat out down a dangerously winding road and deliberately let go of the handlebars. Nothing happened. That experience convinced him that every life has a point. He believes he didn't die because he was destined to use his experience with horses to help people. He believes that's the purpose of his existence. And he's happy.

I don't know what your destiny will be, but one thing I know: the only ones among you who will be really happy are those who have sought and found how to serve.

Albert Schweizer (1875–1965),
German-French missionary surgeon

Try this
Do something generous today for a friend or relative and do something generous for a complete stranger, with no thought of recognition.

Hatred paralyses life; love releases it.
Hatred confuses life; love harmonizes it.
Hatred darkens life; love illumines it.

Martin Luther King, Jr. (1929–68),
American civil rights campaigner

Meditation and spirituality

We've talked about getting out in Nature and experiencing the connection. There is another way. In Chapter 6, we looked at meditation. I said then that your reservoir of inner happiness was actually refilled by your spiritual connection with everything. Now that you've read the 'proofs' I've given above, you'll know that this isn't just a fanciful way of talking. When you reach down into yourself in meditation you're actually reaching out into... what do you prefer to call it? You could say Nature, you could say the Great Oneness, you could say the Divine Consciousness. I'll leave it up to you.

1 *Sitting or lying down with your eyes closed, notice your breathing.*
2 *Without forcing anything, gradually slow down your breathing.*
3 *Make your exhalations longer than your inhalations.*
4 *Empty your mind of any thoughts of past or future.*
5 *Just concentrate on experiencing the present moment that is your breath.*
6 *If any thoughts push their way into your mind just let them drift past; don't pursue them.*
7 *When your breathing is slow and relaxed, notice your heartbeat.*
8 *Without forcing anything, gradually try to think it slower.*
9 *Next notice the sound of your blood in your ears.*
10 *Without forcing anything, gradually try to think it slower.*
11 *In the same way, visit any other parts of your body that you choose.*
12 *Now notice the little dots that 'illuminate' the blackness of your closed eyes.*
13 *Imagine the dots are stars and that you're floating in space.*
14 *Relax your jaw and let your mouth open into a smile.*
15 *What is it that keeps you afloat in space? It is love. You have nothing to fear; love is everywhere, within and without.*
16 *You are in a state of bliss.*

10 THINGS TO REMEMBER

1 *Feeling separate means feeling unhappy.*

2 *You are connected – you'll never walk alone.*

3 *Experiencing and enhancing the connection leads to happiness.*

4 *The atoms in your body came from the stars and have previously been in other people.*

5 *Many scientists believe life on Earth successfully began just once, which means you have a very big family.*

6 *Experiencing the Nature of which you're a part, leads to happiness, but being cut off from Nature not only leads to spiritual unhappiness but physical health problems, too.*

7 *Generosity leads to happiness.*

8 *Involvement in improving the world is empowering.*

9 *We derive our nature through mutual dependence.*

10 *Meditation can be used to create a feeling of bliss by experiencing the essential nature of the universe.*

HOW HAPPY ARE YOU NOW?

Are you feeling more spiritual and, if so, is that making you more happy?

a *Yes.*
b *No, I'm an atheist.*

If you answered '(a)' move on to the final chapter. If you answered '(b)', reflect that atheists can be just as spiritual as people who believe in God. And you can believe in God without following any particular religion. Religions are, after all, codes of conduct and you're perfectly entitled to say you don't entirely agree with any of them. In fact, there's no reason you shouldn't have your very own code of conduct and your very own religion. Read through the five proofs again, take time to think about them, and give your spirituality time to develop.

Keep smiling

The greatest pleasure I know, is to do a good action by stealth, and to have it found out by accident.

Charles Lamb (1775–1834), English essayist

12

....

Your seven-day happiness plan

In this chapter you will learn:
* **how seven days can change your life.**

> *Whatever you can do or dream you can, begin it now.*
> *Boldness has genius, power and magic in it...*
>
> Goethe (1749–1832), German poet

For the next seven days, conduct your life in accordance with the following eight principles. Remember to keep that 'Happiness Diary' as described in Chapter 1.

1 *START THE DAY RIGHT*

For happiness you need 7–8 hours sleep, and you don't want to get up abruptly as this tends to make people irritable. If you possibly can, lay in bed a while before getting up.

While you're contemplating the day ahead, smile. And keep on smiling. As we've seen, by doing so you can actually 'hijack' your body's chemistry. You can smile to make yourself happy, rather than the other way around.

The next thing to do after your first in-bed smile is cuddle. If someone is in bed with you that's the place to start. Aim to cuddle everyone in the household. If you live alone, cuddle your pet. If you don't have a pet, cuddle yourself. Carry on cuddling at every opportunity during the day.

2 BE POSITIVE

The single most important thing you can do to increase your happiness is decide to be happy. Without a conscious effort you'll not improve your 'baseline' level. Remember, it's morally right to be happy (see Chapter 1).

Spend some of that time in bed prioritizing for the day ahead. Don't think in terms of things you 'should' do, or money or status or anything like that. Prioritize instead in terms of the things that give you 'the maximum satisfaction of your whole being' (see Chapter 8). Keep the list short. Instead, aim to maximize the pleasure you get from each thing by really giving it your full attention. Make sure you don't go to sleep without having had an experience that makes the day distinct and gives it a value.

Also make plans for all the wonderful things you're going to do in the coming weeks, months and years. Write them down. Organize them. Look forward to them.

We all need to have the sense that we're progressing. That we're heading somewhere. That 'in every day, in every way, I'm getting better and better'. So learn something new every day. It could be to do with your job, it could be to do with your partner, it could be the name of a star in the sky or a tree in the garden.

Don't take things for granted. Show an interest in everything. Stop to take a look at those flowers. What are their names? How many petals do they have? How does the commuter train work? What kind of engine does it have? How did your taxi driver become a taxi driver? You'll never stop being amazed at how wonderful the world is.

3 NO NEGATIVES

For this week, you're not allowed to complain about anything or criticize anything. And that means in any way at all. So, no scowling, no sighing and no raised eyebrows, either. It certainly

isn't easy (see Chapter 3). But it's a fascinating exercise. It will
a) make you realize how much you complain and criticize, and
b) teach you to find more positive ways of communicating.
Oh, and you're not allowed to criticize yourself.

No negative emotions either. Every day, forgive somebody for
the bad things you consider he/she has done to you. Let go of
all negative emotions by empathizing (see Chapter 4). Defuse
tense situations with laughter. (Practise by reading funny books,
watching funny films and swapping jokes with friends.)

Eradicate all craving for those expensive things you can't afford.
Longing for them is only making you unhappy. Forget about
them (see Chapter 3).

Don't go comparing your partner, your friends and relatives, or
your possessions or situation with those you consider to be 'better'.
Instead, make a list of all the fine qualities of the people around
you and all the things you have to be grateful for; then make
comparisons with people who are 'worse off'.

4 EXPRESS YOURSELF

Be creative. Let the real you be apparent in everything you do.
Begin with your appearance.

Every day do something you've always wanted to do but never
have (see Chapter 8). Don't think only in terms of 'big' things.
'Little' things can generate just as much happiness. And they're
accessible and affordable. Variety is stimulating.

Doing new things may mean overcoming your inhibitions – by
doing the very thing you're anxious about. If there's a particularly
difficult one, break it down into seven stages and tackle one stage
each day.

Cultivate your sensuality – your body is the tool your mind uses
to explore the world. When you eat, really focus on the food.

Savour it. Notice the different tastes. When you walk, notice how your body revels in the movement and how your skin relishes the breeze. When you shower, enjoy soaping every part of your body. For at least an hour listen to music that makes you feel good – don't, for this week, listen to anything that makes you feel sad, however great it might be.

5 IMPROVE YOUR RELATIONSHIPS

Get that oxytocin going (see Chapter 9) by being more tactile (only when it's appropriate, of course). When you shake hands, really feel the hand. Hug. When someone needs support, put an arm round their shoulders. Massage someone close to you and have them give you a massage.

Tell everyone close to you that you love them. Say these words a minimum of five times every day. Empathize.

If you have a partner, bath together, shower together, sleep naked together, massage one another, brush one-another's hair, eat food from one another's lips and reveal 'secret' thoughts. Have sex at least four times during the week. Aim to make it as tantric as possible.

If you don't have a partner, spend time with friends or relatives, talking intimately. The idea is to break down that sense of separateness and put an end to that feeling of being alone. Enjoy practising multiple orgasm techniques on your own (see Chapter 10).

6 LOOK AFTER THE PHYSICAL

Eat plenty of 'happy foods'. But don't try to convert to 'happy eating' all in one go. The body needs time to adjust and it can't be accomplished in one week (see Chapter 5).

If you haven't yet begun an exercise programme get started this week. Take a look at Chapter 7 for ideas on the best way to go about it. You won't be able to get the full benefits in a week, but you should get a taste of the pleasure to come.

7 LOOK AFTER THE SPIRITUAL

Get out into Nature and say 'hello' to your relatives. Don't just admire the view as a spectator. Get right in it. Feel the connection (see Chapter 11).

I'm not going to rush you into getting a pet because it might not be appropriate in your present circumstances. But you need to find a way of interacting with an animal or animals. Maybe you can play with the neighbour's dog, take a riding lesson or help at an animal rescue centre.

Every day, do something generous for a stranger or strangers, without thought of recognition. You could, for example, give money – what you can afford – to a different charity each day. Take time over choosing your charities. Think carefully about the work they do. Savour the impact your donation is going to have. Or you could give time to charity work (an especially good idea if you're feeling lonely).

Spend at least 20 minutes every day on meditation (see Chapter 6).

Take the time to stare up at the night sky, enjoy its beauty and reflect on what an incredible place the universe is (see Chapter 11).

8 REVIEW THE DAY

Just before you go to sleep, replay the day in your mind and note the things you did well and the things you didn't do so well. Don't view it as self-criticism. Simply take note of the day's events and your response to them. Where things didn't go so well, try to work out why, and see if you can work out a better way for the next time. Where they did go well, congratulate yourself. Look forward to the next day with optimism.

HOW HAPPY ARE YOU NOW?

Have you completed your 'seven-day happiness plan' and, if so, is your new score in the questionnaire in Chapter 1 higher than it was?

  a *Yes, I'm happier.*
  b *I've completed the plan but, no, I don't feel any happier.*
  c *No, I haven't followed the plan.*

I hope that you answered '(a)'. If you answered '(b)', are you sure you've really completed the plan and followed all the other practical steps described in the book? (If so, your lack of response suggests you might be suffering from depression, in which case you should consult your GP.) If you answered '(c)' because you haven't followed the plan at all, or haven't followed it properly, then read through it again and implement it. There are no exams and no certificates, but there is a prize – your happiness.

Finally, I leave you with one more quote. These five words of Gandhi's should be the basis on which you live your life. Your very, very happy life.

> **My life is my message.**
>
> Mahatma Gandhi (1869–1948), Indian nationalist leader and pacifist

Taking it further

Books

Beat Your Depression, Paul Jenner, Hodder, 2007.

Emotional Intelligence, Daniel Goleman, Bloomsbury, 1996.

Feeling Good – The New Mood Therapy, David D. Burns, MD, Avon Books, 1999.

Food Pharmacy, Jean Carper, Simon & Schuster, 1989.

Happiness: Lessons From A New Science, Richard Layard, Penguin, 2006.

Happiness: The Science Behind Your Smile, Daniel Nettle, OUP, 2006.

Happiness: Unlocking The Mysteries of Psychological Wealth, Ed Diener and Robert Biswas Diener, Wiley Blackwell, 2008.

Intimate Touch, Michael Reed Gach, Piatkus, 1997.

Men Are From Mars, Women Are From Venus, John Gray, Element, 2002.

Multi-Orgasmic Couple, Mantak Chia, Maneewan Chia, Douglas Abrams and Rachel Carlton Abrams MD, Thorsons, 2000.

Simultaneous Orgasm, Michael Riskin and Anita Banker-Riskin, Hunter House Books, 1997.

Stumbling on Happiness, Daniel Gilbert, HarperCollins, 2006.

Teach Yourself Great Sex, Paul Jenner, Hodder, 2007.

Teach Yourself Massage, Denise Whichello Brown, Hodder, 2007.

Teach Yourself Meditation, Naomi Ozaniec, Hodder, 2004.

Teach Yourself Tantric Sex, Richard Craze, Hodder, 2007.

Teach Yourself the Kama Sutra, Paul Jenner, Hodder, 2007.

The Art of Happiness, HH Dalai Lama & Howard Cutler, Coronet, 1999.

The Art of Loving, Erich Fromm, Thorsons, 1957.

The Complete Body Massage Course: An Introduction to the Most Popular Massage Therapies, Nicola Stewart, Collins & Brown, 2006.

The Endorphin Effect, William Bloom, Piatkus, 2001.

The Happiness Hypothesis, Jonathan Haidt, William Heinemann, 2006.

The Multi-Orgasmic Man, Mantak Chia and Douglas Abrams Arava, Thorsons, 2001.

The New Complete Guide to Massage, Susan Mumford, Hamlyn, 2006.

The Pursuit of Happiness, Darrin McMahon, Allen Lane, 2006.

The Psychology of Happiness, Michael Argyle, Routledge, 1987.

The Science of Happiness, Stefan Klein, PhD, Marlowe & Company, 2002.

The Science of Love, Anthony Walsh, PhD, Prometheus Books, 1996.

The Tao of Love, Jolan Chang, Wildwood House Ltd, 1977.

You Just Don't Understand, Deborah Tannen, Virago Press, 1991.

Websites

authentichappiness.org
Website of Dr Martin Seligman, founder of 'Positive Psychology'.

www.forgivenessproject.com
Advice on how to forgive.

www.pauljenner.eu
Website of Paul Jenner, author of this book.

www.positivepsychology.org
Website of the 'Positive Psychology' movement.

pursuit-of-happiness.org
How to pursue happiness through education.

www.stefanklein.info
Website of Stefan Klein, author of *The Science of Happiness*.

www.stressinstitute.com
Tips on how to avoid stress and how to cope with it.

www.stumblingonhappiness.com
Website of Daniel Gilbert who wrote *Stumbling on Happiness*.

worlddatabaseofhappiness.eur.nl
Data on various aspects of happiness all over the world.

Index

Notes

Notes

Notes

Notes

Notes

Notes

Notes

Notes

Notes

Image credits